SUMMER BIRD FEEDING

by John V. Dennis
illustrated by Irene Brady

THE AUDUBON WORKSHOP, INC.
NORTHBROOK, ILLINOIS
Published by **PRISM CREATIVE GROUP**
CHICAGO, ILLINOIS

DEDICATION

To Mary Alice for her inspiration and to the many Audubon Workshop correspondents who have contributed to the successful completion of this book.

John V. Dennis

TABLE OF CONTENTS

PREFACE

Just this last June, I was relaxing and reading a book while sitting on our deck. The birds were feeding a few feet away. The exuberant chatter of the chickadees and the gossipy twitter of the titmice provided nice background music for my reading.

I could hear the flutter of their wings and feel the slight breeze as they darted over and around me on their way back and forth between feeder and favorite seed-cracking branch. Suddenly I felt movement. I raised my eyes and found myself eyeball to eyeball with a chickadee perched on top of my book. He looked me over for several seconds and then departed for the feeder.

Later, I heard a bumble-bee buzzing behind me, so I turned around to make sure he wasn't going to use my bald head for a landing strip. To my surprise, it wasn't a bee but a hummingbird hovering just behind me—perhaps reading over my shoulder. My turning startled her, and she made a beeline for the hummingbird feeder. After a few deep sips of nectar, she was on her way.

This experience is typical of summer bird feeding and illustrates what Betty and I feel is the major difference between summer and winter feeding. Everyone enjoys watching birds at the feeder on those cold, snowy days of winter; but in that case you are just an observer. In summer when you are out in the yard with the birds, you are more than just an observer—you are a participant in their lives.

In looking for a way to share these joys with other bird lovers, we hit on the idea of a book devoted entirely to summer bird feeding. We approached our favorite author, John Dennis, and asked if he would write the book for us. He enthusiastically agreed. John is an old hand at summer bird feeding, and he has packed his book with solid "how to" information. Through his words and the words of others, he also captures the thrill and challenge of this wonderful hobby.

Al & Betty Nelson
Audubon Workshop
1501 Paddock Drive
Northbrook, Il 60062

Summer bird feeding provides fun for the whole family.

INTRODUCTION

So much has been said about feeding birds in winter and so little about feeding them in summer that my friends at Audubon Workshop decided it was time to remedy the situation. Would I write a book for them on summer bird feeding? I was startled, if not taken aback. For years I had been writing about winter feeding. I had been urging people to start their feeding program in early fall and continue feeding until all danger of late snowstorms was over. Snowflakes and hungry birds went so well together that I felt winter was where the chief emphasis should be. Yet I had always fed birds in summer and had found this to be a highly rewarding time as well. Also I had fed birds in Florida and other places where snow rarely falls. I knew that bird feeding and cold weather did not necessarily go hand in hand. I would have to rethink my notions about when to feed birds.

I decided it was a pity that so many people stop feeding birds because the weather is warmer and many birds are returning to northern breeding grounds. Whether or not birds need our food in summer is a difficult question. A lot depends upon where we live. Where man has greatly altered the landscape, there may not be enough food for birds even in summer. But looking at the reason why I feed birds in summer, I find that it is largely a matter of continuity. I have developed a friendly bond with the tufted titmice, chickadees and nuthatches that have been with me all winter. They recognize me, and I recognize them. I want to keep in touch with them as they begin a whole new round in their busy lives. Courtship, nest building, egg-laying, incubation, young hatching and finally parents attended by young coming to my feeders are some of the activities that lie ahead. The feeding station and bird bath are where I continue to see my old friends. This is where I keep tabs on them and follow their activities.

I am equally pleased to have other guests that have arrived from the tropics or more southern parts of this country. Many of them find my feeders and bird baths. Bright colored and full of song, they add a new dimension to the scene about me. I am now out-of-doors much more. Able to see more and hear more than I could in winter, I have a front seat to the most exciting time of the year. No, I wouldn't lose out on the fun for anything.

I was now kicking myself that I hadn't been the one to have the bright idea about writing a book on summer bird feeding. Here was an obvious gap in our knowledge about feeding and attracting birds. Yes, I would be only too glad to do such a book, but where was I to get the information I needed? Next to nothing had been written on the subject. Although I had fed birds in summer in several eastern states and was now feeding at my home in Maryland, there was still a large part of the country where I had had no personal experience with summer feeding.

Fortunately, Audubon Workshop had an answer to my problem. Thanks to a questionnaire sent to their Helping Hand Bird Club members, I soon had information on summer feeding from forty-nine states and the District of Columbia. No fewer than 725 persons had taken time to answer questions about food, water, birds attracted to feeders, favorite birds, problem birds and problems from small mammals. Without the information contained in the questionnaires, I could not have written this book. In the pages that follow, well over half my material comes from the questionnaires. The rest is from personal experience, correspondence with others who attract birds, and sources in the ornithological literature.

Although Audubon Workshop and I are greatly indebted to Irene Brady for the many excellent illustrations that accompany this book, no one must assume that this book is a field guide. We urge readers to use this book in conjunction with one or more of the good field guides on the market today. Properly identifying the birds at your feeder and bath will go a long way toward helping you enjoy your hobby.

When looking up birds in this book and in field guides, it should be remembered that birds are usually listed in what is known as checklist order. The more primitive birds are listed first, and gradually, showing the changes that have taken place through the evolutionary process, we work our way upward toward more advanced groups. In this book, we begin with the ducks and end with the finches and sparrows.

If readers are confused by more than one name for certain birds, I should point out that periodically a group of ornithologists (members of the American Ornithologists' Union) get together to make any changes that they feel are needed in names of birds and their classification. For example, the cardinal is now the northern cardinal, and four former junco species, including the slate-colored junco, have been merged into a single species called the dark-eyed junco. Changes such as these make it particularly difficult for people who are just learning birds. But we have to live with these changes as best we can. My advice is try to learn the latest names and use them.

In summer you are a participant in birds' lives not just an observer.

CHAPTER ONE

REWARDS OF SUMMER FEEDING

"I feel one misses out on a lot of enjoyment in watching birds by not feeding them in the summer. I have more time to watch birds during the summer and I get a glimpse of what to expect in the winter." That's what Virginia Honaker of Frankfort, Kentucky said in her response to Audubon Workshop's questionnaire on summer bird feeding. Only one of the 725 persons from coast to coast responding to the questionnaire, Virginia expressed a feeling that came out in many of the replies. Feeding birds in summer is an enjoyable activity that shouldn't be overlooked. Why not feed birds in summer? Isn't summer as good a time to enjoy birds as winter? Won't we be helping birds by feeding them at a time when they are overly busy with nesting duties? What disadvantages, if any, would there be in feeding birds in summer?

Both the folks at Audubon Workshop and I have been feeding birds in summer for many years. Others have been doing the same. Indeed, from the earliest days of bird feeding in North America, summer feeding has been an accepted procedure. Through the writings of Florence A. Merriam, a prominent early writer about bird life, we know of year 'round feeding conducted by a lady in Vermont during the 1890's. Florence Merriam herself, on trips to the west with her naturalist husband, fed birds winter or summer wherever she happened to be.

Yet, in spite of proven success in feeding birds in summer over much of North America, the subject has been neglected by authors of books and articles on bird attracting. Winter, with its snow and cold, made such an ideal setting for a bird feeding operation that authors loved to tell about feeding birds at that time of the year. Only when it came to hummingbirds was very much said about summer feeding. Over most of North America feeding hummingbirds is a strictly summertime activity and one that has become ever more popular.

One of the first mentions I have seen of feeding birds, besides hummingbirds, in summer was a short article by Ryan B. Walden in a 1945 issue of *Frontiers*. He stated that summer feeding will bring a variety of new birds to the yard and keep faithful winter residents, such as the downy woodpecker, close by all summer. By having a suet log, he states,we can safeguard young birds that otherwise might have to roam far and wide in search of food and therefore run the risk of being killed by traffic. Walden could have applied the same reasoning to parents and other adults. Long flights expose birds to dangers of many kinds and also sap their energy. Besides using standard bird foods, Walden suggests such extras as melon rind and seeds, oranges, apples, grapes and other fruit. He sums up summer feeding by saying "the cost is small and the pleasures are many."

As Walden suggests, summer feeding is a smaller operation than winter feeding. Normally we will be using less food, fewer feeders, and catering to fewer birds. Early summer may see a few lingering winter visitors in our yard; but for the most part the birds present will be nesting species occupied with such chores as nest building, egg laying, and the feeding and care of young. As the summer residents visit our feeding stations and bird baths, we get to know them and they get to know us. Instead of doing our bird watching through the window, we are now out in the yard much more. Perhaps we are now eating some of our meals outside. Opportunists that they are, birds are beginning to find scraps at

A chickadee stops by to pick a seed off the hat.

our table or are even accepting food from the hand. A much more intimate relationship has developed between ourselves and our feathered clients. We have joined their world. More than ever we are the benefactors of the birds that live near us.

As the summer progresses, we see more and more of the season's young joining their parents at the feeders. The antics of the young, as they learn to feed on their own, provide one of the most entertaining spectacles of the summer months. Before the summer is over, we may see youngsters from second and third broods learning the arts of feeding, flying, and fending for themselves. But by September, the show is largely over. A compelling urge to be somewhere else dominates the activity of birds as summer gives way to autumn. For many this is the time to commence the seasonal migration southward; for others early fall is a time to roam. Even our most faithful year 'round residents may disappear for a while at the end of summer.

Many of us continue to offer food, however. The food is both for late nesters and to let birds know they always have a source to come back to when they are through with their wandering. As stated by Larry Ramsey, one of our Tennessee respondents, "one benefit of summer feeding is that it reassures all birds that our yard is a good place to be."

Is there anything special that we need to know before we embark upon this new adventure of feeding birds during the summer? Will it simply be a continuation of what we have already been doing in winter but on a smaller scale? To provide answers to these questions, with help from my friends at Audubon Workshop, a short questionnaire was drawn up and mailed to members of their Helping Hand Bird Club all over the United States. The ten questions were not only designed for learning facts about summer feeding but also for learning about worries and attitudes. Besides wanting to know which birds responded to food in summer, we wanted to know which ones were "most wanted" and which "least wanted." The answers to these two questions contained some surprises, as we shall see later. Similarly, we wanted to know which mammal visitors were considered to be the most troublesome. The number one trouble-maker was an animal we already knew about — the squirrel. But we were in for surprises when it came to second and third place.

As for questions about food, water and feeders, we were able to confirm what we already suspected; namely, no big changes over the way these items were used in winter were needed but simply better ways of using them. Feeling that we needed to know more about the advantages and disadvantages of attracting birds in summer, we asked if birds drawn to the yard aided in combatting injurious insects, and if they caused any damage to garden produce or flower beds.

Birds received high marks in regard to their services in combatting insect pests. Looking at a sampling of our questionnaire returns, we find mockingbirds in Florida feeding on mole crickets, cardinals in Alabama devouring bagworms, blue jays and cardinals in Kentucky dining on Japanese beetles, cardinals in Ohio eating tomato hornworms, numerous bird species consuming gypsy moths in the Northeast, and starlings ridding rhubarb of slugs in California. The role birds play in freeing our yards of harmful insects couldn't be summed up better than in an appraisal by Sandra Parshall of Virginia. She writes: "robins, jays, sparrows and others spend a lot of time in vegetable and flower beds looking for insects. I almost never have to do battle with insects myself."

Does feeding birds in summer in any way diminish their appetites for insects? Although not a question in our questionnaire, several respondents indicated that summer feeding resulted in more consumption of insects by birds, not less. For example, Esten Davis, in Michigan, stated he noticed a great decrease in damage due to beetles and their larvae since he began feeding birds in summer.

Two factors need to be considered in connection with summer feeding and the benefits we get from birds taking harmful insects. First, people who feed birds usually also provide for them in other ways. The combined effects of plantings, birdhouses, food and water lead to an increase in the bird population. Indeed helping birds through any one of these measures can mean more birds in our yard and therefore more insects being consumed.

A second point to keep in mind is that birds, even the ones that are predominantly seed-eaters, turn increasingly to an insect diet in summer. The white-breasted nuthatch, a vegetarian in winter, becomes so partial

Starlings rid your garden of many pests like this Japanese beetle larva.

to beetles, weevils, ants, spiders, moths and caterpillars in summer that it is only with difficulty that we can keep these comical little birds coming to our feeders. We get the impression that cardinals never tire of sunflower seeds. But I have had these gaudy birds completely desert my feeders in favor of insects and small fruits, such as wild grapes. Scientific studies show that up to 60 per cent of the cardinal's diet is composed of insects in spring and about 40 per cent in summer. It should also be remembered that cardinals, like other largely seed-eating birds, feed their young during early stages of growth almost entirely upon insects.

So far as damage by birds to flower and vegetable gardens was concerned, it came as no surprise that losses of various kinds were reported. After all, some of our fruit and berry crops are as alluring to birds as they are to us. Damage, usually on a small scale, was noted to orchard fruits, such as cherries, apples and peaches. Berry crops suffered from thievery by robins, mockingbirds and others. There were a surprising number of reports of birds pecking holes in tomatoes. In Massachusetts even green tomatoes were not immune from damage of this kind. Grackles, starlings and crows were accused of pecking shoots and blossoms of garden flowers. For example, there were reports of damage to marigolds in the Midwest. For the most part, gardeners took their losses philosophically.

Sharing garden produce with birds was a way of paying them back for all the good they do. As stated by Betty Sharpe from Georgia who had witnessed bird damage to her berry crop — "we really didn't mind though." Gardeners, for the most part, accept the notion of sharing a portion of their produce with birds.

A final question for this chapter is whether birds need extra food in summer. In looking for an answer to this question, we need to consider such factors as weather, population levels, and habitat conditions. A cool wet spring, for example, may drastically reduce the amount of food available to birds in summer — fewer insects and not as many fruits and berries. If the bird population is at a higher level than the habitat can support, starvation may set in. Man sometimes aggravates the situation by over-dependence upon insecticides and clearing the land. Bird mortality due to inadequate food in summer has often been recorded. It is usually the nestlings that suffer.

Birds cope as best they can with limited food supplies. Part of the reason birds establish nesting territories, from which birds of the same species are excluded, is to ensure an adequate food supply for the young. Nesting territories vary in size from half an acre or less for the robin to five or more acres for hairy and downy woodpeckers. Defense of territory is one reason we see many more robins in our yards in summer than woodpeckers.

Unless we are keen students of ornithology and spend time checking birdhouses for signs of mortality, we may never know that food supplies are inadequate. Although we can do little to assist wholly insectivorous birds like swifts and purple martins, we can offer food that will be eaten by a wide variety of other birds. We do this partly for our own pleasure and partly to help ensure a successful nesting season. When parents with young begin to appear at our feeders, we have the satisfaction of knowing we have helped. So enjoy the thrill of summer feeding. In the words of Charlotte Elder, a Kansas respondent: "summer feeding is my favorite time of the year."

A nesting cardinal will be grateful for extra food nearby.

CHAPTER TWO

BIRDS YOU CAN EXPECT

The coming of summer brings new guests to the feeder to swell the ranks of the feeding clientele that are still with us. Many of them, including the hummingbirds, have spent the winter in the tropics or near-tropics. Our guests from the South stay only long enough to nest, raise young, and prepare for the return journey. Other of our summer guests will have travelled shorter distances or will have been with us all along. Thanks to our questionnaire returns, we have a list of 97 bird species recorded at feeding stations in summer. Some, like the blue grosbeak, were recorded in only one state, and others, like the mourning dove, were on nearly every list.

Besides asking for birds seen at feeders, we conducted a popularity poll aimed at finding out which species were rated most highly, and which were at the bottom of the list. Looking at the results of our survey, it was gratifying to see that birds visiting feeders in summer, with few exceptions, were highly regarded. They were praised both for their aesthetic value and their help in controlling garden pests. Scarcely anyone thought feeding birds in summer caused them to reduce their intake of insect food.

The most striking finding in our survey was the species totals found at feeders in summer. These varied from four or five at some feeders to twenty or more at others. Our total of 97 species in all for the United States in summer suggests that, no matter where you live, the birds are there and need only a food supply to become regular guests. The variety we have found in summer must surprise people who begin taking their feeders down in April or May because "there is so little around." Not aware that many resident birds have strayed off looking for nesting sites and will soon be back or that newcomers will be arriving, they decide it is time to quit. Quite the opposite decision should be made! This is as important a time as any to continue supplying food and water. The birds will return. Just give them a little time.

In some parts of the country, if you wait until too late in the year to begin feeding, you may find you have no birds at all. This can occur in far northern regions. Mildred C. Pokorny, who lives in northern Idaho, states that she didn't get one bird at her feeders when she started feeding in winter five years ago. She then began feeding in summer and can now count upon 15 species plus "unidentified sparrows" through a good part of the year. "Now that I feed all year," she states, "the birds know where to come. I value their presence winter and summer."

Winter and summer feeding complement each other. Birds that otherwise might have strayed off stay with us if we feed through the summer. At the same time, feeding birds in winter is an equally good way to hold onto the loyalty of our summer feeding station clientele. By having a more or less permanent population coming to feeders, we attract migrants and nomadic wanderers. A busy feeding station is the best advertisement we can offer to birds passing through our area.

As good a way as any to become acquainted with birds at feeders in summer is to consult any one of the excellent bird guides on the market today. Check species in your area with those I am about to list. You can be sure that you will have some of them in your yard. Range maps in field guides will tell you if a species in question is likely to be in your area. One needs to remember, however, that birds do not always stay "where they are supposed to be." Eastern birds wander westward and western birds wander eastward. One of the greatest excitements at the bird feeder is a stray far from its home range. Strays are more likely to be seen in fall and winter than in spring and summer.

I particularly like the Golden Series *Birds of North America* by Chandler S. Robbins and co-authors. It treats *all* North American bird species. Following the A.O.U. checklist order, as I do in this book, the bird guides start with more primitive birds and continue up the evolutionary scale until the most advance group is reached. In terms of feeding station birds, this means starting with the ducks and ending with sparrows.

DUCKS, PHEASANTS, QUAIL, PIGEONS, AND ROADRUNNER

Only a few feeders tabulated in our survey were visited by ducks. Mallards were reported as summer visitors at several midwestern feeders, and the wood duck was present at an Ohio feeder. Ducks are greedy eaters that normally accept food only on the ground. Seldom do they stray far from water.

The California quail, a jaunty-looking bird with a topknot, should be looked for at far western feeders. Coveys containing 25 to 60 or more birds sometimes descend upon feeders in winter. During the summer breeding season, these large coveys are replaced by family groups containing a single pair and their young. Parents, along with small chicks, can be seen at feeders any hour of the day.

When California quail find a ground feeder, they will visit regularly.

The northern bobwhite, like the California quail, no longer arrives in large coveys as summer approaches. A pair or two may be seen feeding on food scattered on the ground. After the young hatch, parents will spend their time helping the young in finding insect food. Most of our reports of bobwhites at feeders in summer came from the South.

The ring-necked pheasant, more often present in winter, appeared at feeders as widely separated as Oregon and New York and a few states in between. Like the two species just mentioned, the ring-neck doesn't linger but eats quickly and departs.

Soiling the ground and taking more than its share of the food, the pigeon is greatly disliked by many. Complaints about pigeons were chiefly from urban areas. The best way to discourage visits from these street scavengers is to withhold food. By keeping food well off the ground in hanging feeders, we can hold onto our preferred customers and put a stop to inroads by greedy pigeons. Hanging tubular feeders should be equipped with trays or there will be enough spillage to satisfy the needs of pigeons — birds that do their feeding on the ground. Although seldom welcomed at bird feeders, pigeons do enjoy a fair amount of popularity in city parks.

A favorite bird of mine, the mourning dove, won less approval than I expected. More people in our questionnaire poll disapproved of this sometimes scrappy bird than approved of it. Too many mourning doves arriving at one time and monopolizing feeders seemed to be the basis of the complaints. Unlike the pigeon, the mourning dove can feed at trays on hanging feeders. But the bird is too large to balance itself on the small perches of tubular feeders and eat from the feeding ports.

Easterners travelling west are always thrilled by their first glimpse of the roadrunner. These days this striking looking bird is found not only on the wide open plains but is increasingly at home in yards and gardens. Here they are tolerated but not always liked. They have predatory habits and sometimes harm garden plants. A California respondent tells of roadrunners eating green tomatoes. The roadrunner also responds well to bits of meat tossed its way.

HUMMINGBIRDS

Hummingbirds are well liked by everyone. If an economic reason were needed to convince people about them, one should remember that they perform a valuable service in pollinating flowers. Our respondents reported eight different species coming to sugar-water feeders. Hummingbirds ranked fourth in popularity — only the cardinals, chickadees and bluebirds received more votes. I treat the not- always-easy art of feeding hummingbirds in chapter 8.

WOODPECKERS

Woodpeckers are much less in evidence during the summer months, but this is not because they have moved away. Most woodpeckers are permanent residents. They are quieter in summer and half hidden in the foliage of the trees in which they live. Any that are nesting in the near vicinity will continue visiting feeders if suitable foods are offered.

Offer suet in summer to attract the downy and other woodpeckers.

Altogether seven species of woodpeckers were recorded by our respondents at feeders in summer. The most exciting of these was a pileated woodpecker at the feeder of Wilmer B. Bates in Ohio. Red-headed woodpeckers were reported at feeders in twelve midwestern and southern states. The acorn woodpecker, a close relative of the red-head, was reported at feeders in California and Arizona. Other woodpeckers reported included the flicker, red-bellied, hairy and downy. The downy, the smallest of them all, was by far the most popular according to our poll. All the woodpeckers received high marks for their services in ridding trees of insect pests.

JAYS AND CROWS

The jays, like the pigeons and doves, did not fare well in our popularity poll. Some of us, myself included, take delight in having these colorful birds; others, rightly or wrongly, accuse them of robbing the nests of other birds. Taking too much food and monopolizing feeders are still other complaints. The blue jay at feeders in the eastern half of the country and the scrub jay at feeders in the western half are the most common species. The Steller's jay, found chiefly at higher elevations, was listed at feeders in eight western states. Barely qualifying for inclusion in our summer feeder list were the pinyon jay at a New Mexico feeder and the gray jay at a Montana feeder.

The blue jay won praise for devouring gypsy moths and Japanese beetles but was accused by several of pecking holes in tomatoes. We had one report of blue jays nipping buds off marigolds and zinnias. Jays in the West were criticized for damaging garden plants.

The American crow and its western relatives — the black-billed magpie and Clark's nutcracker — are regarded with suspicion by bird lovers because of their nest robbing proclivities. Reports from our respondents indicate these three species are occasional visitors at feeders in summer. A minor complaint against the crows came from an Illinois respondent who said the birds picked off flowers from the petunias!

Titmice visit in early spring, leave to raise a family, then return for summer feeding.

CHICKADEES AND TITMICE

No one has any doubts about this group. Universal favorites, the chickadees and titmice continue at feeders through the summer but usually in smaller numbers and with occasional absences. Ina Nafziger in Illinois states that chickadees, tufted titmice, and white-breasted nuthatches abandon her feeders for a period each spring; then they return bringing their young with them. Temporary departure is a common occurrence if nest sites are not available in our yard or nearby. This is a good reason to place nest boxes for cavity nesting birds.

Only cardinals had a higher rating than the chickadees in our questionnaire popularity contest. The titmice, represented by the tufted titmouse in the East and plain titmouse in the West, were not far behind in popularity. Summer feeding stations in the West were often patronized by anywhere from one to three chickadee species and many times by the plain titmouse. Our artist, Irene Brady, whose home is in an upland region of southwestern Oregon, plays host in summer to the mountain, chestnut-backed, and black-capped chickadee. Like many of us, she feels these friendly birds deserve extras at our feeders no matter what the season. Whether they have food at feeders or not, the chickadees and their close relatives never cease their endless search for tiny insects.

Westerners, blessed with more kinds of chickadees than we in the East, have still another friendly little bird. It has the ways of the chickadee. This is the bushtit, a midget of a bird that often travels in large flocks. Although uncommon at feeders, it was reported in summer at feeders in Washington, Oregon and California.

NUTHATCHES

The nuthatches, such an important part of the winter feeding station flock, will stay with us in summer if food and nesting sites are available. Instead of being a part of the flock, the nuthatch in summer is on its own. It comes and goes on a schedule that is tied to feeding a mate or young in the nest. Visits at feeding stations are only long enough to seize a morsel of food and fly off with it. The white-breasted nuthatch is the best known of four species that visit bird feeders. But our western respondents have provided us with many reports of red-breasted nuthatches at feeders in summer. Sally Spaulding of Elmira, Oregon has a pair that nest in a birdhouse in her front yard and come to bird feeders behind her house bringing their young with them. The pygmy nuthatch was reported at feeders in Arizona, Colorado and Montana. Another very small nuthatch, the brown-headed, has a more eastern range and was reported at feeders in summer in Maryland, North Carolina, Georgia and Alabama. Well liked by everyone, the nuthatches took sixth place in our popularity contest.

BROWN CREEPER AND WRENS

The brown creeper is one of the least assuming of all feeding station birds. Along with other north-bound migrants, it disappears from most parts of the country in the spring. But in mountain areas, particularly in the West, this small, drably colored woodland bird is present the year 'round. Feeders in the state of Washington were visited by brown creepers through the summer.

When living in South Carolina one summer, I built a temporary bird feeder out of cinder blocks. A pair of Carolina wrens acted as though

I had built the feeder just for them. They were in and out of cavities in the blocks all day, and, from time to time, sampled food in the tray on top of the blocks. A large wren of eastern North America, the Carolina can be expected at bird feeders throughout the year. Less likely visitors in summer are the house wren and Bewick's wren. Although both were reported at feeders by our respondents.

Wrens will fill your yard with their bubbling song if you put up houses in several locations.

MOCKINGBIRD, CATBIRD, BROWN THRASHER

More given to song than eating in summer, the male mockingbird fills the air with its melodies day and night. The mockingbird along with its two close relatives, the catbird and brown thrasher, are unpredictable when it comes to food at bird feeders. Seeming to go out of their way to avoid the confusion at the bird feeder, the three find ways to obtain food without having to join the throng. The mockingbird often chases the other birds away and then eats. The catbird comes to special feeding places we have established for it, sometimes taking food from the hand. The brown thrasher furtively dashes out from the shrubbery and retrieves food that has fallen to the ground.

We have reports of brown thrashers at feeders in summer from ten states. Like the mockingbird and catbird, the brown thrasher is fond of fruits and berries. A complaint was voiced by a gardener in Ohio that brown thrashers pulled newly sprouted corn; others reported damage to tomatoes by thrashers. On the other hand, an Illinois respondent told of brown thrashers turning over leaves to get at earwigs. In terms of popularity, the three species rated highly, the largest number of votes going to the mockingbird.

ROBIN AND BLUEBIRDS

On our lawns looking for worms and nesting in our shade trees, the robin makes itself at home wherever we may happen to live. Usually indifferent to food at feeding stations, the robin seems to need a special invitation before it will accept our handouts. We can sometimes win it over with fruit, raisins or bakery products. Catherine M. Spears in Wisconsin has had as many as 35 robins at once coming to raisins. Other respondents, from Rhode Island to California, have been successful in luring robins with food in summer.

In spite of its fondness for tomatoes, fruits and berries of all kinds, the robin has a tolerably good economic record. We have a report from Massachusetts telling of a female robin feeding over 100 grubs to her young in fewer than two hours. An Indiana report tells of robins eating tomato hornworms and one from Rhode Island of robins devouring gypsy moth caterpillars.

Not generally regarded as a feeding station bird, the eastern bluebird was nevertheless reported at feeders in four states — Georgia, Alabama, Tennessee and Arkansas. The bluebirds, including two westerners, the mountain bluebird and western bluebird, are close to the top of the list in terms of popularity. Only the cardinals and chickadees received higher ratings. Beautiful, gentle and in need of help, bluebirds deserve the best we can offer them. I'll be discussing ways of helping these often hard-pressed birds in my final chapter.

WAXWINGS

More easily attracted by fruits and berries in ornamental plantings than food at feeders, cedar waxwings and their western cousins, the Bohemian waxwings, are rare visitors that seldom stay long. In summer, we can hope for only the cedar waxwing and only if we live in more northern states. Trim, mannerly and looking as though dressed for a formal occasion, the cedar waxwing is apt to be the most elegant of our visitors to feeders or bird baths. We have summer records of cedar waxwings at feeders in Oregon, Idaho, Wisconsin, Iowa and New York.

CHAPTER THREE

MORE BIRDS
YOU CAN EXPECT

A s we continue our review of birds that visit feeding stations in summer, we may have begun asking ourselves if the feeder flock in summer is really so different from the one we had in winter. The answer to this question will depend a great deal upon where we live. If winters where we live are mild — not drastically different temperature-wise from summer — chances are we will not see big changes in the composition of the feeder flock. Several of our respondents from coastal regions of the Far West report they have about the same birds winter and summer. E. Glazier, who lives in the San Francisco area, states, "we feed all year 'round and winter isn't much different here from summer." Farther north in Washington, Gloria M. Hull also notes few differences. She says, "I have almost the same birds at my feeders all year long and simply note an increase in numbers after the young begin arriving in summer."

In many other parts of the country, there are striking differences between winter and summer. This is particularly true where winters are cold and summers hot. In more northern states, there are winters when feeders are inundated with northern finches. They come in such numbers that it is difficult to supply food fast enough. The evening grosbeaks,

Black-headed grosbeaks are welcome summer migrants in the West.

purple finches, pine siskins and others that make up these winter flocks sometimes move quite far south; in the East, reaching down to Florida and the Gulf Coast. Sometimes the northern birds do not return to their northern breeding grounds until May or June: therefore, we may have them for a while in summer. In Massachusetts in June, I have seen evening grosbeaks at the feeder along with male indigo buntings and such other summer birds as the northern oriole. The contrasts in color were dazzling!

In northern parts of this country and also in mountain regions, certain of the northern finches breed, and we can look for them winter or summer. It can be seen, therefore, that there is no clear division between winter and summer guests. But birds making up what can be called the tropical element do furnish a major difference. The arrival of hummingbirds, vireos, warblers, orioles, tanagers, southern grosbeaks and buntings in April and May do make for some of the biggest changes in the year. Another big change occurs when birds in the same group depart in late summer and early fall. Not all of the far south visitors will attend bird feeders or use bird baths, but we can offer hospitality and hope for the best.

THE STARLING

By far the most unpopular bird in our questionnaire poll, and generally in disrepute everywhere, the starling has few friends. Since its introduction to our shores in 1890, it has spread to every part of this country and has appeared far south and north of our borders. Its faults range from dirty, noisy roosts to competition with other birds at feeders and usurping nest sites of cavity-nesting birds.

Yet the starling's record is not all bad. If we look at the starling's food habits, we will find good reasons to excuse the bird for some of its faults. Studies show that in April, May and June, 90 percent of the starling's food consists of injurious insects — chiefly weevils, grasshoppers, June bugs, potato bugs, crickets, locusts, Japanese beetles and beetles of other kinds. The starling's taste for insects tends to keep it away from feeders during the summer. George Shiras, III, writing for the National Geographic Society in 1935, noted a sudden change-over in starling food habits in the spring. The starlings that had been such a nuisance at his feeders suddenly began searching for insects in flower beds and on the lawn. Once they began doing this, they had no more use for food at feeding stations.

Many of us, myself included, rarely, if ever, have starlings at our feeders — winter or summer. Marty Murphy in Washington states that in 13 years she has encountered only one starling, and the bird was pecking at a slug. Mrs. Hans Miller in Rhode Island, putting in a good word for these "much- maligned birds," says she is grateful to them for cleaning Japanese beetles off her roses and raspberries. By withholding soft foods such as kitchen scraps, fats and bakery products, we can keep starling competition at our feeders to a minimum.

WARBLERS AND HOUSE SPARROW

Warblers are the small, colorful birds we see little of except when they pass through on migration, and they normally do not frequent feeders. However we do have reports of yellow warblers at feeders in Montana and California; pine warblers at feeders in Alabama and West Virginia; and American redstarts at feeders in Connecticut. By far the best way to attract warblers to our yards is to have bird baths, especially ones in which the water has a ripple effect created by a drip or fountain.

Having arrived in this country before the starling, the house sparrow, our other best know import from Europe, has had more time to make enemies. But its numbers today are only a fraction of what they were earlier in this century. In many parts of the East, the house sparrow is no longer a pest at bird feeders. This is not so true in grain-producing areas of the mid-central states where the house sparrow is still common. The best way to discourage house sparrows from coming to bird feeders is to withhold favorite foods. These include bread, wheat, corn and seed or grain mixes.

Like the starling, the house sparrow does help us by reducing populations of harmful insects. Our respondents credit it with consuming Japanese beetles, gypsy moth caterpillars and grasshoppers. But these services hardly make up for its many faults. Bird lovers object to the way it takes over nesting sites of cavity-nesting birds and harasses them even if it can't enter the opening. Only the starling and grackle had lower ratings in our popularity poll.

MEADOWLARK, BLACKBIRDS, GRACKLE, AND COWBIRD

Primarily insect-eaters of open grasslands, meadowlarks rarely visit bird feeders. But we did have reports from California and Iowa of western meadowlarks eating at feeders during the summer.

The red-winged blackbird, more of a seed and grain eater than the meadowlark, and also Brewer's blackbird, a western species, do show up at feeders winter and summer. No one seemed to object to either species *per se*. But many did object to birds they simply called "blackbirds." I am inclined to believe that many people group nearly all very dark or nearly black in color birds under the heading "blackbird." These may include the crow, starling, grackle, cowbird and the two species just mentioned. Also the rusty blackbird, reported in summer at an Ohio feeder, fits into the group that many simply call blackbirds.

Whether we like them or not, the blackbirds make up a very important part of feeding station flocks. If anything, blackbirds are more in evidence in winter. Sorting out still more members of the group, we come to the common grackle, close to the bottom in our popularity poll. Only the starling had a lower standing.

Parading about as though it owns the place, the common grackle makes a nuisance of itself by eating more than its share and crowding out other birds. Sometimes it is a killer. One of our questionnaire participants wanted to know what bird it was that decapitated house sparrows in her yard. Most likely this was the common grackle. At times, they go on killing sprees that are largely directed against house sparrows.

Its population booming and audacity increasing, the common grackle is becoming a number one problem at bird feeders. The best way to keep this aggressive bird in check is with anti- grackle type feeders. This is a topic that will be discussed in my chapter on bird feeders.

Holding fourth place in low esteem is a bird most of us do not seriously object to at feeders so long as it does not arrive in large flocks. This bird, the brown-headed cowbird, is disliked primarily for its parasitic habits.

The female, in a carefree manner, deposits her eggs in the nests of other birds and lets them do all the work. Usually selecting nests of much smaller birds, she will, as a rule, deposit one egg in each of the nests that she borrows. Sometimes she removes the eggs of the rightful owner. Even if she doesn't, the young cowbird grows faster and eats more food than its small nest mates. As a result, they are often crowded out and die. If we see a small sparrow or warbler feeding a bird five or six times its size, we can be sure we are seeing a foster parent attending to the needs of an ungainly young cowbird.

ORIOLES AND TANAGERS

We leave our troubles with grackles and cowbirds behind us as we greet bright colored birds from the tropics that begin arriving in late spring. If we are lucky, we may have a pair of orioles nesting near us. While busy weaving their pendant nests, they provide us with song, bright color, and visits to the bird bath and feeder. The wide-ranging northern oriole is our most likely guest. Jean Bancroft of Winnipeg, Canada has had as many as three pairs of northern orioles nesting in trees in her yard. She provides six-inch lengths of white string and yarn as nesting materials for the birds. Baskets with halved oranges, attached to limbs of trees, serve as feeders for the orioles.

In the East and also as far west as Texas, we can sometimes count on the orchard oriole. Scott's oriole and hooded oriole are possibilities in parts of the West. As might be expected, the orioles received a good rating in our popularity poll.

As if the orioles hadn't already provided enough color, we still have the tanagers with their jet black, vivid reds, and greenish yellows. The two species reported at feeders in summer by our participants were the western tanager and summer tanager. Like the orioles, the tanagers are with us only for the summer; then, after completing their nesting duties, they hurry back to the tropics which is their real home.

Orange halves provide an enticing snack for a northern oriole.

CARDINAL AND PYRRHULOXIA

Fortunately we have many colorful birds of our own that are with us the year 'round. At the top of the list is the northern cardinal whose cheerful song and friendly habits make it a favorite of nearly everyone. Our respondents voted this their favorite bird by a wide margin. The one or two pairs that hold territory in our yard are the birds we will see at our feeders through the summer. Along with them will be offspring from successive nestings. Since cardinals may have as many as four broods in a nesting season, it isn't long before there are many more cardinals in evidence than the original ones.

A plentiful supply of food at feeding stations does not diminish the cardinal's appetite for insects. Our respondents reported cardinals feasting upon bagworms, Japanese beetles and tomato hornworms. Other insects on the cardinal's bill-of-fare include grasshoppers, caterpillars and bugs of various kinds. So tempting are natural foods that cardinals will slow down on their visits to feeders during the summer.

From the Southwest we are reminded that part of the country has two cardinals — one is the species I have just mentioned and the other is a close relative, the pyrrhuloxia. Much like the cardinal in appearance but not as brightly colored, pyrrhuloxias are shy birds that normally do not come into yards or visit feeders. But William A. Davis of Tucson states that pyrrhuloxias in his yard act about like cardinals, except that they don't sing from so high up in trees. They come to both grain and sugar-water in his yard.

GROSBEAKS

Hardly have we said good-bye to the wintering evening grosbeak than another grosbeak, resplendent in black and white attire and with a rosy breast, arrives to take its place. The male rose- breasted grosbeak is one of the most strikingly colored birds to be seen at bird feeders. The female, as in so many bird species, is more soberly colored. She must not attract attention to herself while she sits on the nest. The rose-breasted grosbeak, with a northern nesting range, and the black-headed grosbeak, with a western one, are summer visitors that add more than their share of color and excitement to the feeding station scene. Rose- breasted grosbeaks are reported at feeders in eleven states stretching from Massachusetts to Minnesota. The black-headed grosbeak is reported at feeders in seven states stretching from Oregon to New Mexico.

In bidding good-bye to the evening grosbeak, I neglected to say that, in mountainous parts of the West, the northern Great Lake states and New England, this handsome grosbeak stays on to breed. In summer, as in winter, it is a frequent visitor to bird feeders. Respondents in nine states, including ones as far apart as Vermont and Oregon, reported evening grosbeaks at their feeders in summer. In 1960, there was a surprising mid-July record of one at an Alabama feeding station!

The blue grosbeak, in a way as striking in appearance as any of the others, rarely visits bird feeders. The one record we have for this species at a feeder in summer is from Utah. Like the rose-breasted and black-headed, this grosbeak spends the winter in the tropics.

Rose-breasted grosbeaks add color and excitement at eastern feeders.

BUNTINGS

Smaller, daintier birds than the grosbeaks, the buntings comprise another group of colorful birds from the tropics that often appear at feeding stations in summer. Their common names give us a hint of the colors they display. The indigo bunting, found widely in summer in eastern North America, does, in the adult male, have a deep indigo-blue plumage. Ravenously hungry upon returning north in the spring, indigo buntings sometimes feed steadily for long periods at bird feeders. Later they may desert feeders for a diet composed of insects and other natural foods.

The lazuli bunting, a beautiful member of the group that breeds in the West, is drawn to feeding stations to about the same degree as the indigo bunting. We have reports of this bunting at feeders in Utah, Montana and Oregon.

The most brightly colored bunting of all is the painted bunting of the deep South. Reports of this bunting at feeders come from Florida, South Carolina and Texas. The male is so vividly striking in its red, blue and yellow-green plumage that even the word "painted" doesn't do justice to its colors. Another name — nonpareil, "unequaled in splendor" — seems more appropriate. Once the painted bunting or nonpareil accepts a feeder, it becomes an almost constant visitor. Young follow parents to feeders containing millet and other small seeds. Lucky are those who succeed in attracting these gorgeous small birds to their feeders!

FINCHES

In areas where ranges overlap, we may have difficulty in deciding which of three similar-looking finches we are seeing. Cassin's finch, difficult to distinguish from the purple finch, is a far westerner reported at feeders in summer in Idaho, Montana, Utah, Arizona and New Mexico. The purple finch, rosy-red in the male (not purple), is much better known as a winter visitor. Nevertheless, it is a bird to look for in summer at feeders in the far West and also in northeastern states. When feeding birds in Massachusetts in summer, I had the company of dozens of purple finches gobbling sunflower seeds and clamoring for more as the supply dwindled.

We are so used to hearing about the spectacular way in which the starling and house sparrow spread throughout North America that we almost forget that one of our native birds is in the process of doing much the same thing. The house finch, the third of our look-alike finches, is no longer limited to its native western range. An eastern population, beginning with birds released in New York City in 1940, has moved into all of the eastern states. Only three or four years ago, the house finch was only a winter visitor at my feeders in Maryland; now it is my most common feeder guest the year 'round.

What has happened at my feeders has taken place at thousands of other feeders in the East. Complaints are being heard about house finch greediness and the way it sometimes usurps feeders from other birds. On the whole, however, people like this peppery little finch that holds its own and seems to be rapidly replacing the house sparrow. A good song-ster and far more handsome than it's rival, the house finch is meeting with a fair amount of approval. Our popularity poll showed more people in favor of the house finch than opposed to it.

Before moving on to the smallest of the finches, I shouldn't com-pletely overlook two finch-like birds that few of us ever see. The pine grosbeak, reported at feeders in summer only from Montana and Minne-sota, is, for the most part, a northern bird whose range dips southward into the Rockies. The male looks like an over-sized purple finch. The other, the rosy finch, is found in high western mountains and was reported at feeders only in Montana.

PINE SISKIN AND GOLDFINCH

For those of us in the East who think of the pine siskin solely as a winter visitor, it may come as a surprise to know that in much of the West, the pine siskin is a year 'round resident. Just as eager for food in summer as in winter, it has a way of over- running bird feeders and dispossessing other birds — large and small. For birds this small (less than 5 inches in length) to win out, suggests a determination hard to match in the bird world. We had reports of pine siskins at feeders in summer from ten west-ern states stretching from Montana to Arizona. There are also reports of pine siskins remaining at summer feeders in the Midwest.

The pine siskin's close relative, the American goldfinch, is not as domineering but just as given to swarming all over feeders containing their favorite foods. It is a special treat to have goldfinches at the feeder in summer. The male, resplendent in its black and yellow plumage, and the

Niger seed attracts finches and pine siskins like a magnet.

female, also looking brighter than in winter, add all the color we could ask for. We also had reports of the lesser goldfinch, a western species, coming to feeders in California and Oregon during the summer. The goldfinch, like all "finches," received high ratings in our popularity poll.

By finches, people can mean anything from goldfinches to house finches. We can only conclude that the group as a whole are welcome visitors. If there is any complaint about the goldfinch, it has to do with the sudden departure the birds make at almost any season of the year. More will be said about this in the final chapter.

TOWHEES, JUNCOS, AND SPARROWS

Look for towhees on the ground. The wide-ranging rufous-sided towhee keeps as much as possible to dense shrubbery and, now and then nervously flitting its tail, ventures forth to sample food that has fallen to the ground. A far bolder bird, the brown towhee of the West spends much of its time in the open. It is a common sight to see this rather non-descript brownish bird out on lawns and even venturing out into streets. Still another western towhee, the green-tailed, can be expected at western feeders.

The junco, so much a winter bird that it is called "snowbird," is scarcely to be expected at many feeders in the summer. But we did have reports of the Oregon race of the dark-eyed junco at summer feeding stations in California, Oregon, Washington, Idaho and Montana.

After our winter sparrows and juncos have returned north in the spring, we often feel a sense of loss. Luckily the gap is, to some extent, filled by the arrival of sparrows that have spent the winter in more southern parts of the country. The chipping sparrow, the most friendly of all our sparrow guests, may nest in our yard and patronize our feeders. A less likely visitor, the field sparrow, may wander in from grassy fields which are its real home. Parts of the West and Midwest can count upon white-crowned and fox sparrows in summer. And the song sparrow, as much of a joy in summer as winter, is in and out of bird baths and on the ground below bird feeders throughout the summer months.

SELECTIVE FEEDING

This brief resume' of summer feeding station visitors should give us an inkling of the opportunities that await us if we will only continue our feeding program. Do not become discouraged when the winter sparrows and juncos leave. By continuing to feed, we hold onto the patronage of permanent residents and also win over birds that are beginning to reach us from farther south. If, during our feeding program, we attract birds with dubious reputations, we can either love them, as many say they do, or we can make a few changes in our menu and the types of feeders we use.

As I point out in my chapter on food, both safflower seeds and this-tle are greatly relished by many of our favorite birds. On the other hand, the two seeds rate poorly with lesser liked birds and also squirrels. But no matter how unpopular a food may be, *it will be eaten if nothing else is available*. Therefore continue offering less expensive foods such as mixed bird seeds. A food of this kind will distract unwanted guests and keep them from feeders reserved for birds that rate more highly.

The shy rufous-sided towhee ventures out of hiding to scratch for scattered birdseed.

CHAPTER FOUR

RAISING THE FAMILY

B y feeding birds throughout the year, we witness an unfolding drama that in early winter begins with courtship behavior. By late spring our feeders are stages where we see a wide variety of behavior connected with courtship, mating and nesting. Many of the same displays continue through the summer. The final act in this drama is young at feeders being fed and taught how to feed by parents. Still another drama is about to unfold — in many species flocks begin to form and the migratory urge takes hold.

Donald and Lillian Stokes in their guides to bird behavior state that, by establishing feeders, we are provided with endless opportunities to see birds communicate with each other. The feeders, they say, attract birds to our property and increase the chances they will remain to nest. I am indebted to the Stokes' guides for much of the information I have about courtship and other nesting season behavior. This is something we may miss if we stop feeding birds at winter's end.

COURTSHIP BEHAVIOR

We can start looking for first stages of courtship behavior in early winter or perhaps even earlier. In what are called behavior calendars, the Stokes outline periods of the year when different behavioral activities can be looked for. As seen in these calendars, courtship behavior may extend from early winter into midsummer. In some species courtship begins even before winter is well underway.

The pigeon, whose courtship displays begin in November, and the house sparrow, whose displays begin in January, are among the first birds to exhibit signs of the mating instinct. Somewhat later, in February, we begin to see examples of courtship behavior in the downy woodpecker, blue jay, white-breasted nuthatch, starling and cardinal. March sees courtship getting underway in the mourning dove, chickadee, tufted titmouse and brown-headed cowbird.

Why do we see these early overtures when nesting, as a rule, does not get underway until April or later? The answer is that birds, like other higher organisms, need to find mates and hold them. To overcome competition and woo his perspective mate, a male has to stake his claim early in the season. In nearly all birds, the males go through a series of ritualized performances that seem calculated both to impress the female and intimidate other males. These include bowing, bill pointing, fluffing out feathers, quivering wings and a variety of calls. Each species has its special rituals. These may be quite varied, as in the mourning dove and pigeon, or all but lacking as in the robin.

Once a male has made progress in wooing his intended, he has little reason to relax. He must guard her from other suitors and continue his courtship until she finally gives in to his advances. Copulation, followed by nest building, egg laying, incubation, hatching of eggs and rearing of young, are only the first rounds in a busy nesting season. Most birds nest more than once. The mourning dove may have anywhere from two to five broods in a single season, and the cardinal anywhere from one to four broods. To hold his mate, the male may continue to sing and conduct courtship until the end of the nesting season. In some species, the male takes turns at incubating eggs and in brooding and feeding young; in other species, the male, in a carefree manner, leaves most of the nesting duties to his mate.

Viewing courtship and nesting behavior from our windows in winter as well as from the yard as the weather becomes warmer, we are able to follow events from earliest stages until the season ends in late summer. The place to watch is the bird feeder. Here we see a dramatic change in behavior by the male cardinal. Instead of chasing his mate from the feeding tray as he has been doing through early winter, he begins offering her choice bits of food. As he brings her a sunflower seed that he has shucked, she crouches with her beak open and wings quivering. Turning his head sideways, he places his offering in her mouth. The scene is an almost exact duplicate of what occurs when parents feed their young. The young birds also crouch and vibrate their wings.

At the same time courtship feeding is getting underway, male and female cardinals are singing duets. The male may begin a song, and the female, from another part of the yard, will complete it. Antiphonal singing, as it is called, continues in the cardinal well into the nesting season. Like courtship feeding, it is a way to cement the pair's bond.

Courtship feeding is seen in other feeding station birds, including jays, titmice, chickadees, white-breasted nuthatches and evening grosbeaks. Besides being a courtship ritual, feeding of the female by the male may be a prelude to more important duties later on. In many species, the male, even though he may take little part in nesting duties, does feed his mate. When we see a male cardinal flying off with food in its bill before the young have hatched, we may be sure the food is for a mate on her nest. Later food from the feeder will be taken by both parents to young in the nest.

A male cardinal offers its mate a choice seed during courtship.

The mourning dove, the Stokes remind us, is a marvelous bird to watch at feeders because most of its courtship behavior is conducted there. Of five types of courtship behavior listed for the mourning dove, one of the most striking is known as the "bow-coo." The male makes a low bow, almost touching the ground with his head; he may do this a number of times. This is followed by a long "coo" with head raised. This performance is to impress the female and warn away would-be suitors. When the female is ready for copulation, she may be seen inserting her bill inside the male's partly open bill while both birds bob up and down.

The mourning dove's "bow-coo" courtship is reminiscent of the chivalry of old.

The common grackle, one of the least popular birds at bird feeders, to some degree makes up for its unruly manners by putting on ludicrous performances at and near the feeders. The male seems to outdo himself in his efforts to impress the female. He fluffs out his feathers, spreads his wings and tail and approaches his intended with head down and bill pointed to the ground. She couldn't be less interested. She may either attack him or walk off as though completely oblivious to his overtures. Eventually she will respond to his attentions; both take part in initial nest construction. But he soon leaves all the work to her. Many times at this stage the male will wander off and find a new mate.

Nesting responsibilities do not weigh heavily upon the brown-headed cowbird. As we have seen, the female deposits her eggs in the nest of other birds, and, with this done, goes on to lead a carefree existence. But the courtship antics that precede egg-laying are as elaborate as in the grackle. The male, as in the male grackle, approaches his beloved with feathers fluffed, neck arched, tail and wings spread. In the climactic part of his performance, he seems to topple over head first. Not quite hitting the ground, he rights himself and begins a series of calls that sound like water bubbling out of a bottle. None of this seems to impress the female. If the pair is at a feeding station, chances are she will go right on eating with her back to him!

PARENTS FEEDING THE YOUNG

As nesting activities get underway, our interest begins to shift from courtship behavior to occupied nests in and around our yard. For the most part, out-of-sight and hard to reach, the nests are so well hidden that we may never know they are in the yard. But we do have a clue as to approximate locations when parents fly away from the feeder with food in their beaks. After a period of ten days or so, the parent bird may be seen flying off in other directions carrying food. We can assume that the young have left the nest and are being fed wherever they have gone. Sooner or later, they may follow parents to the bird feeder.

Sometimes we wonder, as we watch the intensive feeding that is going on, whether parents always single out safe foods to bring their young. Would they perhaps be fooled by something that looked like a food they were used to? Probably not! Tests conducted in England on food preferences of titmice showed that they had a strong preference for white foods. This was in line with their liking for white grubs and white foods at feeders, such as suet. The experimenter went on to say that "apparently any whitish object put out close to a regular feeding place is tested for edibility..." But soap placed at feeding places was "immediately and unanimously rejected" after birds took one to five pecks at it.

This is not to say, however, that parents can always be trusted in regard to the foods they feed their young. Turning once again to British authorities, we learn from Len Howard in her book *Birds as Individuals* that a few nestling titmice seem unable to digest fat. She thought mutton fat in large quantities was harmful to young birds. But she knew of only one case of mistaken choice of food for the young.

A second worry from England — this time reported in a 1972 issue of the journal *Birds* — is related to titmice feeding their young on peanuts, coconuts and other items rich in fats and oils. Young could not always digest foods of this kind and mortality resulted. On our side of the Atlantic since peanuts are not a standard bird food and coconut is rarely if ever used, there is little danger of harm from the foods mentioned. But one should use caution in supplying parents with peanuts and peanut butter when young are in the nest.

A nest full of young keeps this catbird parent busy providing enough to eat.

After reading about the misgivings that our British friends have about certain foods, I like to think back to an early observation of mine about a catbird feeding its young. Each time the bird came to the feeder, it would take a raisin from a feed tray and then hop over to a small dish containing peanut butter. Dropping the raisin, it would pick up some peanut butter in its bill and place it on top of the raisin. Then it would fly off with the raisin and peanut butter "sandwich" to feed young in a nearby nest. I couldn't help but think that this bird was smart enough to provide its young with a balanced diet consisting of more than one ingredient! Isn't it reasonable to suppose that most birds do this instinctively and that our worries about wrong food choices are largely groundless?

DANGERS OF THE NESTING SEASON

Of bigger concern during the nesting season are the many tragedies that occur — nests blown down, birds hitting windows, birds trapped in buildings, a parent or the young killed by a predator. We can help prevent some of these calamities. If nothing more than restricting the movements of dogs and cats when young birds are in the yard, we will have helped increase the youngs' chances of survival. Pasting a silhouette of a small hawk on a window that birds sometimes hit will reduce loss. Birds that do hit a window and are only stunned should be kept in a darkened container until they revive. Release the bird out-of-doors by gently taking it from the container and letting it fly off as you open your hands.

Many times birds almost miraculously escape dangers without there being any intervention on our part. I recall reading in an old issue of the ornithological journal, The Auk, how a mother junco in a yard in Juneau, Alaska was flushed off a nest and directly into the mouth of a waiting cat. The cat was pursued by a dog and thereupon released the junco. The junco returned to her nest and successfully raised a brood of five. When living in Florida, I was told how a cat, after seizing a young mockingbird, was attacked by the parent bird. In trying to ward off its attacker, the cat opened its jaws and the young bird flew off unharmed. If we should see a cat holding a live bird in its mouth, we can try one of two ways to make it release the bird. One way is to shout at the cat and give it a tap on its nose. The other is to slightly squeeze the cat's throat.

HELPING CHICKADEES

Sometimes we are overly solicitous and "rescue" young birds that should be left where they are. But more on this later as I recount the story of a lady who, after a career as an opera and concert singer in Chicago, began feeding birds and watching over the fortunes of birds that nested in her yard. Her efforts supply an example of what many of us can do to help birds during the nesting season.

Miss Jeanette Urbain of Seattle, Washington kindly tells us some of the problems she had in attracting birds to her small yard only ten minutes from downtown. When she moved to her new home from Chicago four years ago, she did not have one bird in her yard — not even a house sparrow. After she put up a bird feeder in September, she soon had a pair of chickadees that stayed on to nest the following spring. Other birds came too. In three years her yard list had grown to 35 species.

The pair of chickadees that nested in a birdhouse outside her bedroom window became objects of special interest as she watched over their fortunes. Through differences in behavior and a slight difference in appearance, she learned to tell the male from the female. She watched as they built a nest inside the house and took turns incubating the eggs. Both parents stayed in the house at night. When the young hatched in mid-May, the parents took turns bringing them small pieces of suet from the bird feeder. Owing to a very wet season, there were very few insects about. Therefore, the lives of the young birds may very well have depended upon the food they received from the feeding station.

At first the young were fed every half hour, but as they became older, they were fed at longer intervals. About two weeks from the time the first egg hatched, Miss Urbain had the thrill of seeing "a little head peering out of the entrance hole." Shortly, one of the youngsters left the house and flew to a tree. Three other youngsters left the house soon after-ward. All could fly perfectly, but the parents had to direct them where to go. After the young were out of the nest, the family disappeared for two weeks. Miss Urbain worried about what had happened to them, but was relieved to finally have all six return to eat at her feeders.

Black-capped chickadee brings its fledglings to the feeder as soon as they can fly.

Following the fortunes of this brood and a second one later in the summer was an absorbing pastime. Although everything went smoothly the first year, the chickadees had their troubles the following two years. The most serious problem occurred the second year, when, true to form, a male house sparrow, unable to squeeze through the entrance hole, took it upon himself to prevent the chickadees from using the house. Finally, after four days of constant shooing by Miss Urbain, the stubborn bird gave up and the chickadees were able to nest and bring off another brood.

BIRDS IN DISTRESS

Many small problems, such as that of the house sparrow blocking the entrance hole to the birdhouse, can be solved with patience and imagination on our part. But what are we to do if we find an injured, sick or orphaned bird that needs care? Early summer, with so many young birds leaving the nest, is a particularly difficult time of the year from the standpoint of birds in distress. Unless we have state and federal permits to keep protected bird species in captivity, we may be in trouble with the law if we take such a bird into our custody for any length of time.

Luckily there is a growing movement in this country and also abroad that concerns itself with looking after birds and other wildlife that need special care. The parent organization is the International Wildlife Rehabilitation Council, P. O. Box 3007, Walnut Creek, California 94598. At its centers are facilities for looking after the many kinds of wildlife species that have been rescued and brought in for care. Wishing to know more about these centers, I visited the one closest to me. This was the Chesapeake Wildlife Sanctuary at Bowie, Maryland where, towards the end of summer, I observed hundreds of birds being cared for.

Dianne Pearce, the director, gave me a tour of the farm house and barns on the property where the "patients" were housed. I especially wanted to know what the center's policy was toward rescuing supposedly orphaned young birds. Many times people see a small bird, not yet able to fly, on the lawn or perched somewhere and conclude that it has been deserted by its parents. Unless something is done quickly, they feel, the young bird will fall victim to a cat or some other predator. Dianne gave me two good rules to follow in handling such cases: 1. If possible, bring any cats or dogs indoors and advise people to stay away from the immediate vicinity of the young bird. 2. Observe the young bird continuously for an hour or more to see if a parent bird comes to it. If no parent appears, then bring the bird indoors and seek help from a wildlife rehabilitation center.

Once the young bird has been brought indoors, it should be kept in a cardboard box or other container and fed at frequent intervals. The type of food to offer depends upon the species of bird. If possible, you need to properly identify the young bird (not always easy with fledglings) and seek advice on what it should be fed. According to Dianne, young of many species, including young purple martins, thrive on a diet of water softened high protein kitten or puppy pellets. She advised that an unfeathered bird should be fed every half hour and a feathered one every hour. Food should be supplied through the day from sunrise to sunset. Young birds recently out of the nest cannot feed themselves. Food should be gently placed in the bird's mouth. Do not try to give the bird water.

Hopefully, after phone calls to the state game department or Audubon Society, you will have the young bird in safe hands in a day or two. Once the young bird has learned to eat on its own and is able to fly, it will be released back into the wild. I know from personal experience in banding birds that hand-raised youngsters do stand a good chance of survival. Some of those that I banded returned to my yard in later years. However, injured birds may never be able to adjust to the wild again. Larger birds with permanent injuries, such as herons, hawks and owls, may be given a home at a zoo or nature center.

As for the young bird that does have parents but has prematurely left its nest, you should make every effort to find the nest and return the bird to it. If you aren't careful, the youngster may immediately jump out again. But if you cup your hands over the nest and hold them there for several minutes, the youngster will usually settle down and stay where it is.

We cannot expect the nesting season to go by without some losses. When we realize, for example, that the American robin lays 3 to 4 eggs and has two to three broods in a season, we can see that there is a safety margin in numbers. Birds have large broods in order to compensate for the many losses that overtake the young and also the parents. Our emphasis should be upon correcting hazards attributable to man. These will range from toxic garden sprays to birds hitting windows and becoming trapped in buildings. I would also include helping native birds when they face threats from the introduced house sparrow and starling. I can sympathize with Miss Urbain and her troubles with the male house sparrow.

YOUNG AT FEEDERS

Even though we may experience problems during the course of the nesting season, we can always count upon a crowning event of the year. This is the appearance of young and their parents at our feeders. If we have prepared ourselves for very small birds, half the size of their parents, we will be in for a shock. With the exception of families of small chicks, seen in pheasants and other fowl-like birds, the newcomers will be approximately the same size as their parents. We will recognize them by stubby tails, feathers with wisps of fluffy down, and table manners that remind us of very spoiled human children teasing their parents. Within days the downy look, except for fluffy ear- tufts, will be gone. For a while, the youngsters will have an owl-like look. When the last of the down is gone, the young bird will look almost exactly like the adult female.

If anything, the table manners will worsen. Begging, with mouths wide open and wings fluttering, they so pester the parent that we begin to feel sorry for this hard-pressed bird. At a feeder well stocked with suitable foods, the parent is able to jam down food in every gaping mouth. But this does not stop the insatiable youngsters from clamoring for still more. The parent will try to escape by flying away. This doesn't always work. Squawking and screaming, the youngsters pursue the frantic parent as it disappears into the foliage. Ruth Horcher in Florida tells how young cardinals at her feeder would beg for food from the father amid much squawking and fluttering of wings. Then, when the parent was not looking, they would feed themselves.

We can understand why Elizabeth Doyle in Michigan feels that "nothing is more satisfying and pleasurable in summer feeding than watching cardinals feeding and teaching their young and downy woodpeckers feverishly doing the same."

Though they still beg, the Steller's jay must teach its young to feed themselves.

CHAPTER FIVE

SUMMER FOOD SELECTION

B efore drawing up a menu for our summer guests, we should bear in mind that we are now competing more than ever with natural foods. Our offerings will need to be as tasty and nutritious as the foods that birds find in the wild. But the feeding station does have one big advantage over natural food supplies — *birds know where to come.* They don't have to travel as far or expend time and energy searching for the often hidden and hard-to-find foods that exist in the wild. This is a big advantage to birds that are fully occupied with nesting duties.

The foods we offer birds at this critical time of the year should be ones that are rich in protein, vitamins and minerals. Parents and young alike need the lift that comes with energy-giving, concentrated foodstuffs. This is why foods like sunflower, thistle and suet remain popular with birds even after natural foods have become much more plentiful. To a large extent the foods we offer help round out diets that otherwise might be lacking in certain elements. By taking some of our foods and rejecting others, birds tell us which ones they crave and need.

ARE CHANGES NEEDED?

Will birds keep right on eating the same foods we have supplied all winter, or do we need to make changes in our menu? Beth Johnson from Colorado puts this question somewhat differently after commenting she was interested in feeding in summer to help keep birds nearby and nesting. She states, "we are not sure what to feed or how to feed."

To help Beth Johnson and many others who are not sure about summer feeding, I have gone to questionnaire results and other sources to find out which foods are most suitable for bird feeding at this time of the year. No fewer than 636 respondents supplied information on the foods they used in summer. Judging from this response, there are a wide variety of foods being used. So let us look at these foods and see which ones are best suited for your birds and your part of the country.

SEEDS

Contrary to what we may expect, seeds used in bird feeding do not lose their appeal in summer. Many of our respondents reported that they continued supplying the same seeds they used in winter and had good results with them.

The number one seed, winter or summer, is sunflower. No fewer than 65 per cent of our respondents reported using sunflower in summer. The kinds used included striped seeds, black oil seeds and sunflower meats or hearts. Black oil seeds, which have gained steadily in popularity, offer two big advantages over other kinds. Thanks to a soft outer husk, the seeds can be readily opened by small birds, and 70 per cent of the seed is meat in contrast to only 57 per cent in striped seeds. For sunflower with no husk at all, we can go to sunflower meats. Well-liked by goldfinches and other small seed-eaters, the meats, with their absence of hulls, are the answer to feeding birds and producing the least amount of litter. Nothing is wasted with sunflower meats.

Birds seem drawn to sunflower seeds partly because of taste and partly because of their exceptional nutritional value. As stated by Alan Pistorius in his book, *Birding and Bird Attraction*, "sunflower has three times the iron, twice the calcium and phosphorus, and half again more potassium as hamburger." He goes on to say it provides an equal amount of protein and twice the fat (the other energy producer) and a fair amount of carbohydrates. He adds that sunflower is a better supplier of vitamins than hamburger.

Furthermore, this ideal seed for bird feeding can be used in any part of the country — no matter what the climate or season. It is as popular with birds in the South or Southwest as it is in more northern sections.

A second seed, quite close to sunflower in appearance and nutritive content, is safflower. Practically unknown in bird feeding until a few years ago, safflower is becoming increasingly popular because of its

A large feeder attracts Carolina wrens, chipping sparrows and song sparrow.

selectiveness. It is well received by many of the birds we'd rather have and poorly received, or not eaten at all, by competitors such as starlings, grackles and squirrels. At my feeding station in Maryland, safflower was popular with evening grosbeaks and purple finches in winter and it is a year 'round favorite with tufted titmice, chickadees and cardinals. The only complaint I've heard about safflower is that it often takes birds a long time to recognize the seeds as food. To overcome this problem, all you need to do is mix some sunflower seeds with the safflower. Birds will soon be eating both.

Many people are not yet on to safflower and its potential as a lead-ing bird food as seen by the fact that only 12 per cent of our respondents were using it as a summer bird food. Most of this use was in the Midwest.

Better known and more widely used than safflower is a small black seed that looks like the caraway seeds used in some bakery products. This is niger, better known as thistle. It is an oil rich seed imported into this country from Ethiopia and India. Originally used as a food for cage birds, thistle suddenly began to enjoy great popularity in outdoor bird feeding when it was discovered to be an ideal food for small finches and, at the same time, little liked by most competitors, including the starling, house sparrow, red-winged blackbird, grackle and squirrels.

I have found thistle to be the most popular food we can offer the goldfinch. There have been occasions when no goldfinches were coming to my feeders; I offered thistle seed in a standard thistle feeder, and, in less than a day, goldfinches suddenly appeared. It sometimes seems uncanny the way they respond to a fresh offering of these seeds. Almost always, mourning doves will gather below the thistle feeder to feed upon fallen seeds. Doves are one of the few larger birds to have a taste for them.

Thistle is as popular with small finches in summer as in winter. One of our Michigan participants reported using more thistle seed in summer than winter. Twenty-nine per cent of our respondents reported using thistle in summer. The greatest use was in the Northeast followed by mountain states in the West.

Judging from questionnaire results, mixed bird seeds have slipped in popularity from a few years ago. Only 40 per cent of our respondents used mixed seeds — far fewer than the 65 per cent using sunflower seeds. A common complaint is that not all the ingredients in the mixes are eaten. This is especially true if the mix contains sizable quantities of less popular seeds and grain. Some suppliers are aware of the complaints about waste and now offer more sunflower, cracked corn and popular kinds of millet in their mixes. Such inferior ingredients as flax, rape, oat groats and buckwheat are no longer seen in any quantity. Red millet is being replaced by the more popular white or white proso millet.

Whether used in mixtures or separately, the more popular seeds and grain are now standard foods that most of us use without hesitation in feeding birds.

The millets, best used on the ground or in platform type bird feeders, are well received in summer by doves, the brown-headed cowbird, red-winged blackbird and song sparrow; in winter by most of the sparrows and finches. Eight per cent of our respondents reported using millet in summer (chiefly white proso millet), and the greatest use was in the Midwest. There were only a few reports of canary seed being used. Since the mineral and protein content of smaller seed, such as the millets and canary seed, is not high, they should be used with other more nutritious foods.

Hungry mourning doves gather beneath the niger feeder to clean up spills.

GRAIN

The grains, including corn, milo, oats, wheat and barley, are members of the grass family and rate highly as food for poultry, livestock, and, when processed, for the human race. Once widely used in bird feeding, the grains have been overtaken by better foods, such as many of those already mentioned. Only corn, in any of its many forms, is still used extensively as a bird food. A good heat and energy producing food, corn is best suited for winter feeding. Nevertheless 14 per cent of our participants reported using corn in some form in summer. Corn is chiefly offered to birds as fine or medium cracked corn and only rarely as whole corn or corn on the cob. Corn on the cob, as reported by a Wisconsin respondent, is well received by red-headed woodpeckers.

Although I wouldn't delete corn from the summer feeding menu, I would suggest using it sparingly. Cracked corn spoils easily, and I question the wisdom of feeding sizable amounts of this high carbohydrate grain to birds in hot weather.

PEANUTS AND PEANUT PRODUCTS

What I have said about corn also applies to the underground tubers we call peanuts. A wholesome food, rich in protein and calories, the peanut and its by-products are better suited for winter feeding. Questionnaire results show that this food is not heavily used in summer. Only 9 per cent of our respondents reported using peanuts in any form in summer.

Sandra Parshall in Virginia commented that she offers only the number of peanuts that birds can eat right away. "Otherwise they turn rancid." Barbara Wise in Wisconsin, noting that birds know what is good for them, states that they take fewer raw peanuts as the weather becomes warmer. A Minnesota respondent, recognizing the limitations of the peanut as a bird food, stated that "peanuts are really meant for squirrels."

Except for limited uses, such as feeding jays, squirrels and inviting birds back to a feeder or to a new feeder, it would seem best to limit the use of peanuts in summer. But, as observed in Michigan, raw shelled peanuts at any season are excellent bait to bring birds to a new feeder. They invite woodpeckers, chickadees, titmice, nuthatches, cardinals, grosbeaks and towhees. Peanut hearts, the bitter germ of the peanut left over in the manufacture of peanut butter, is often offered as a bird food. However, these small tidbits are, on the whole, poorly received by most birds. Finally, as I mentioned in chapter 4, the British question the safety of the peanut as a food for baby birds.

SUET AND SUET MIXES

Although many of our respondents reported problems with suet in summer, no fewer than 32 per cent of them used suet in some form. This made suet the third most popular food for summer with only sunflower and mixed seeds ranking higher. The popularity of suet lies in its appeal to nearly all birds, including a number that are dominantly insect-eaters. Young birds recently out of the nest are often introduced to suet feeders by parents. Here they receive what is the equivalent of an insect diet — a protein-rich food, high in calories, which aids them in attaining rapid growth and which gives them the extra energy they so greatly need at this stage of their lives.

To provide birds with all the advantages that come with suet, we need to take special precautions to prevent this food from melting or becoming rancid. If possible, we should use beef kidney suet. This is the hard white fat from around beef kidneys. It resists heat and rot better than any of the other suets. But regardless of which suet or suet mixture we use, there are proper ways to use these foods in summer, and I am grateful to our participants for their suggestions.

To keep suet from melting, suggestions range from using it in holders in shady situations to putting the suet in a freezer each night. Mrs. Hans Miller in Rhode Island puts her suet out only early and late in the day. She times her offerings to visits made by nuthatches and woodpeckers. Conveniently, the visits of these patrons are normally in the cooler hours of the day. When the suet is not being offered, she keeps it in the refrigerator.

The off and on exposure of suet may seem like a lot of extra work. But the advantages of doing this seem to out-weigh the inconvenience. We should keep our suet fresh and solid by indoor refrigeration, and, very important in many areas, keep it indoors at night where it will be out-of-reach of possums, raccoons and other nocturnal prowlers. Many of our respondents told how marauding animals at night not only went off with the suet but destroyed the holders as well.

Suet is often rendered and mixed with other ingredients. We can make our own suet cakes using such extras as seeds, raisins, peanut butter, flour, cornmeal and brown sugar. One can also purchase suet cakes containing extras of various kinds. There is even a suet cake that is fortified with insects remains. Tests are underway to see if cakes with dead insects in them are better liked by birds.

To simplify our transfer of suet from indoors to outdoors, we should use suet holders that can be hung from the eaves or a tree branch by means of a nylon cord or link chain with a hook at one end. When we are ready to bring the suet indoors, all we need to do is lift the suet feeder from its hook and bring it into the house.

A suet feeder adds protein rich food for a hairy woodpecker nesting nearby.

BAKERY PRODUCTS

Better suited for winter feeding, bread, as well as other bakery products, should be used sparingly in summer. Use of such products in summer should be largely limited to getting birds to come to a re-acti-vated feeder or a new one. Non-seed eaters often respond better to bread than any other food. Bread can also be used in small amounts as nourishment for baby birds. At a feeding station in California, bread soaked in milk was offered as a food for northern orioles feeding their young. Throughout the nesting period parents came to a bowl holding the bread and milk and flew off with this food to their nest. When the young had fledged, they were conducted to the bowl by one of the parents. After each of five youngsters had its share, the parent would take a swallow or two before leaving.

Although high in carbohydrates, bread and other bakery products do not offer birds a great deal from a nutritional standpoint. Therefore these foods should serve only as a taste treat, or, for a brief time, as food for young birds. The addition of milk made the bread being fed to the young orioles a richer and more palatable food.

Nine per cent of our respondents reported using bread in their summer feeding program and one per cent used doughnuts. These foods were normally used with other more nutritious foods. If bread, it should be white bread. Whether fresh or stale, birds seem to crave it. But never offer birds moldy bread and do not leave bread at feeders long enough for it to become moldy.

FRUIT

Seldom used in bird feeding in winter, fruit takes on greater importance as birds from the tropics begin to arrive for their summer stay. Many of them, including orioles and tanagers, have been eating fruit in their winter home and therefore respond well to such fruits as oranges and bananas. More northern birds are better tuned to eating apples. Whatever fruit we offer, it should be sliced in half. This will make it easier for birds to eat. Impale the fruit halves on twigs, nails or any other handy object. Halved orange was used in summer by 7 per cent of our respondents, halved apple by 4 per cent and raisins by 3 per cent. A few other fruits, including pears, grapes and bananas, were used sparingly.

Judging from these results, fruit, if anything, is under-used in summer bird feeding. One can only guess that people become discouraged when birds fail to respond promptly to fare of this kind. Also there are such drawbacks as messiness, decay and flies if fruit is left out too long. But we can avoid problems of this kind with dried fruit. Raisins and currants are popular with the same birds that accept fresh fruit. If softened by soaking or steaming, dried fruits are much more palatable to the birds that eat them.

One summer a pair of catbirds were in the habit of coming to a dish containing raisins I allowed to soak in water overnight. The same kind of offerings go well with the mockingbird, robin, bluebird, cedar waxwing, oriole, scarlet tanager, summer tanager, cardinal and rose-breasted grosbeak. Birds like the juice as much as the raisins. In summer a large share of the raisins is used by parents to feed their young.

MISCELLANEOUS FOODS

People seem much less inclined to use odds and ends in feeding birds in summer. This is not so true in winter when cold weather prevents spoilage. Only six of our participants reported using kitchen scraps in summer, only five reported offering birds dog food, and only one offered cheese. Adding a few other items to the list, including popped popcorn, melon seeds, nuts and cranberries, we find that miscellaneous foods were used by only 5 per cent of our respondents.

In a way, it is too bad people aren't more experimentally inclined in summer. This is the season when parents are feeding young. We can cater to nestlings with some of the foods already mentioned (suet, bread soaked in milk, softened raisins); in addition, we might want to offer a few other soft, moist foods. These could include cottage cheese, cornmeal mush, cooked oatmeal and small fruits and berries. Mealworms, if we are willing to go to the trouble of raising them, are the perfect answer to feeding insectivorous birds and their young.

An apple stuck on a twig is a favorite snack for robins.

Sugar-water, a category all its own, was widely used according to our questionnaire results. Although generally considered to be a food only for hummingbirds, it is widely used by other birds. I will have a lot more to say about this popular beverage in my chapter on hummingbirds.

RULES

1. Check seeds or grain being purchased to be sure they are free of weevils.

2. Purchase seeds or grain from a reliable distributor. Buy only as much as birds will consume in 4 weeks. Food stored for longer periods of time in summer may spoil or become contaminated with insect larvae. An exception is safflower seed which ordinarily resists decay and insect damage for six months or more.

3. Store in moisture proof metal trash cans with tight lids. This is to keep out rodents and reduce chances of spoilage. Plastic trash cans are sometimes subject to squirrels chewing holes in them.

4. If a new food at a feeder is not eaten right away, don't give up. It takes time for birds to recognize a new food.

5. Remove stale or slightly spoiled food from feeders every few days and replace with fresh. This also applies to food in tubular hanging feeders; it, too, can become moldy.

6. In hot weather, suet and suet mixes should be kept under refrigeration

except for the periods when they are exposed at bird feeders.

7. Do not put more food on trays or on the ground than birds can consume in a day or two. It is best to provide fresh food daily.

8. Most food should be kept high and dry in hanging feeders. This is especially true in regions of abundant rainfall.

Cowbirds and a red-winged blackbird find seeds in a weathered fence rail.

CHAPTER SIX

SUMMER FEEDER SELECTION

L ooking at the other part of Beth Johnson's question, "how to feed in summer," it can safely be said that there is no longer such a great urgency. Winter cold and snowstorms are a thing of the past. Therefore we no longer need tight, weather- proof feeders that protect both food and birds from the elements. Emphasis is now upon feeders that allow us to have an unimpeded view of the birds themselves.

Ways in which to make this change-over are reflected in comments such as those made by Charlotte McKibben in Montana; besides using some of the same feeders she used in winter, she turns her deck into a feeding station. Nancy K. Hughey of Virginia uses hanging feeders as well as a large flat platform on the railing of her deck. Here she can watch the antics of birds and squirrels almost at arm's length. She enjoys the squirrels as much as she enjoys the birds.

Feeding on a deck or balcony is commonplace for many because they do not have a yard. This is true of Winnie B. Morton in Tennessee who lives in a second floor apartment with a balcony sheltered by a hackberry tree. Making the most of this space, she has arranged her feeders to limit competition between the birds that use them. During the summer over ten species come to her balcony feeders.

Limited space does not dampen attendance at a unique bird feeding station at the Cornell Laboratory of Ornithology in Ithaca, New York. In an area about half as large as a tennis court are a variety of hanging feeders suspended from the limbs of a large mulberry tree. Below the tree is a split-rail fence, no doubt brought there to give the area a rustic look and serve as a bird feeder. The top railings have rotted out along their upper surfaces leaving convenient hollows into which cracked corn and mixed birdseed are poured. The feeding area is hemmed in on one side by a lake and on two sides by the laboratory building. Visitors, watching from behind large plate glass windows in the building, can look out at waterfowl on the lake or take in the bird feeders.

A mixed assemblage of birds use the feeders. Ducks and geese paddle up from the lake to join chickadees, blue jays, cardinals and house finches at the feeders. Land and water birds ignore each other, but I did observe Canada goose goslings jabbing at black ducks and mallards with their bills. The ducks and geese fed either on grain scattered on the ground or clambered up onto the split-rail fence to feed. House sparrows, grackles and red-winged blackbirds fed almost anywhere. Cardinals, the boldest birds of all, fed on a narrow window ledge where only a quarter of an inch of glass separated them from the human viewers inside. Blue jays and chickadees, along with gray squirrels, for the most part fed at tubular hanging feeders suspended from a line between the mulberry tree and the building. The menu at the many feeders consisted chiefly of black oil sunflower seeds but also millet and cracked corn.

Judging from the comments of viewers and how some of them couldn't seem to tear themselves away from the window, there was something spell-binding about the scene in front of them. If anything, the squirrels stole the show. Hanging head-down with hind feet clasping the top of tube feeders, squirrels, three and four at a time, could be seen eating at metal reinforced feeding ports. After filling up, a squirrel would often hang by its toes from the bottom of the feeder before dropping to the ground. It almost seemed as though they were playing to the audience.

NUMBER OF FEEDERS

A good question to ask, as we get ready for summer feeding, is how many feeders will be needed? Dorothy Simon in Wisconsin, who has large numbers of cardinals and goldfinches at her feeders throughout the year, uses twelve feeders in winter and six to eight in summer. But most of us, myself included, find that we can get by with fewer feeders than this in summer. As a rule, we may need two or three feeders for seeds, one or more for suet, and, if we are feeding hummingbirds, enough sugar-water feeders to accommodate the numbers that are coming to our yard. We may also find it advisable to scatter seeds and grain on the ground.

Making a comparison between early spring and mid-summer, I found that I was using only about half the amount of sunflower seeds in mid-summer and less than a third of the thistle seed that I had been using earlier. With the departure of pine siskins in early May and most of the goldfinches by the end of the month, the rate of food consumption had fallen off markedly. Through the summer, birds take about the same amounts of food daily at my feeders. But in winter and early spring, amounts taken daily fluctuate quite widely. Cold weather and especially a snowfall see many more birds than usual at the feeders.

A white-breasted nuthatch easily uses a feeder for clinging birds only.

It seems likely that the trends I have noted are repeated at bird feeders nearly everywhere. The best policy, it would seem, is to begin summer feeding with approximately the same number of feeders used in winter and early spring. If birds are not emptying the feeders as quickly as before, take them down one by one until you have the right number to meet the needs of your clientele.

PLACING FEEDERS

In summer it is no longer necessary to place feeders where they will be sheltered from cold winds. The main consideration now is finding a location where the birds can be easily viewed by us and where they will have cover in case of attack by predators. This means we need to survey our grounds carefully. First we should check locations where feeders can easily be seen from our deck, patio or windows. Will these locations be too open, or are there trees or shrubs growing nearby? So long as the plants do not block our view, they are important assets. Besides providing shade and cover, they may offer branches from which to hang feeders and perches where birds will await their turn.

If, as is often the case, there is not a suitable branch from which to hang our feeder, we still have several options open to us. Many of the plastic tubular feeders on the market today can be mounted on light-weight metal poles. In some models, the poles are driven into the ground; in others, the pole is attached to a heavy, movable base. In either case, the feeder with its pole can be moved periodically until it is in exactly the right location for us and the birds. A second option is to attach a line between two trees, or the house and a tree, and suspend the feeder from the line. I have two hanging feeders attached to a line suspended between a flowering dogwood and the house.

If we do not have trees or shrubs in the right places near our feeders, I suggest planting a few. Nurseries offer tree-sized specimens, or we can plant fast-growing trees and shrubs that will soon provide all the cover that is needed. Some fast- growing deciduous trees to consider include larch, silver maple and mulberry. Dense cover, so important to birds as a refuge, can be provided by planting shrubs. Among those that are fast- growing and which furnish good cover are autumn olive, bush honeysuckles, viburnums, barberries, deutzia and multiflora rose.

MAMMAL COMPETITION

Not everyone is as willing as the Cornell Laboratory of Ornithology to give free license to squirrels and let them eat all they want to. Nevertheless, many of our respondents had no reservations about feeding any hungry form of wildlife that might happen to come along.

Several stated that all God's creatures were entitled to help and sympathy.

It seems likely that many people take up bird feeding with generous impulses such as those expressed in the last paragraph. But when a small mammal begins monopolizing a feeder eating more than it really needs, then begins chewing the feeder apart, we lose our patience.

In our questionnaire, we asked for opinions about mammal visitors to feeders. Squirrels, the red, fox, flying and especially the gray squirrel, came in for the greatest criticism. Having a disapproval rating of 36 per cent, the squirrels were by far the most unpopular small mammals.

Hanging an ear of corn helps keep gray squirrels away from other feeders.

Strangely enough, second on the disapproval list was the chipmunk. Cute animals with clever ways, the chipmunks arouse resentment by hauling off and eating more than their share of the food. But with a disapproval rating of only 9 per cent, the chipmunks can't be said to be in general disfavor. The same is true of the raccoon whose disapproval rating was 8 per cent. Midnight forays that leave bird feeders, including hummingbird feeders, empty and lying on the ground are behind the raccoon's tarnished popularity.

In a category all by itself, the house cat got by with a disapproval rating of only 5 per cent. Widely condemned by bird lovers at one time because of its inroads upon bird populations, the house cat seems to have made a partial recovery from the low image it once had. Perhaps there are many fewer cats on the loose these days.

Possums with a disapproval rating of 3 per cent and rabbits with a rating of 2 per cent could hardly be said to represent much of a problem at bird feeders. Barely mentioned were rats, skunks, woodchucks, dogs, deer and black bear. Deer were accused of knocking over feeders and eating some of the food. A black bear near Duluth, Minnesota sampled food at a bird feeder for several nights and then wandered off.

Not everyone reported success in using baffles and squirrel-proof feeders to stop thievery by these wily mammals. But successes seemed to far out-weigh failures. Donald G. Cornell in Pennsylvania announced he had beaten the squirrel problem with feeders such as the Mandarin and Big Top and a post feeder with a small trash can inverted just below the feeder. He stressed the importance of keeping feeders well away from trees and other places from which squirrels can jump. Cliff Garrison of Quincy, Illinois states that he experimented with squirrel-proofing for 15 years before hitting upon a practical solution. Just when he had decided that a squirrel's ingenuity and persistence exceeded his own, he discovered a simple solution. This was to apply a generous coating of Vaseline to the metal post to which the feeder was attached. Fresh Vaseline, he states, needs to be applied only 2 or 3 times a year. He adds, "scores of times over the years, I have watched a squirrel climb eagerly and hopefully up the post until he reached the treated area, whereupon he would slide slowly downward with a look on his face that is completely inde-

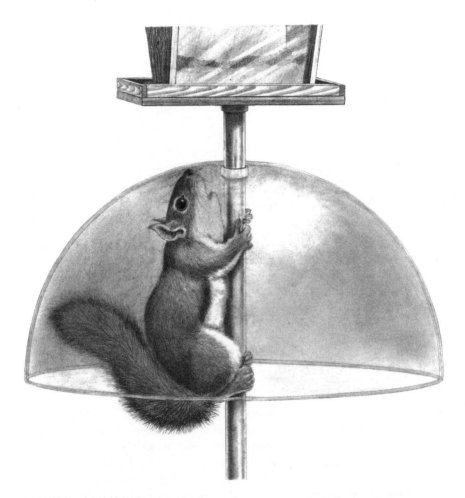

The right squirrel baffle keeps this red squirrel off the feeder.

scribable.'' Squirrels have amazing jumping skills. They jump upward from the ground to heights of over four feet and many times this distance from vantage points such as rooftops and limbs of trees. Feeders should be out-of-range of jumping-off spots and so strongly made that squirrels, if they do reach them, cannot chew them apart. Generally speaking, it is much easier to deal with a squirrel on the ground than one in a tree or on a rooftop. The squirrel that jumps downward, with gravity on its side, can perform amazing feats.

Bribery helps with squirrels and other mammals. By establishing mammal feeders well away from bird feeders, we reduce their appetite for bird food; and, at the same time, we may find ourselves with an enjoyable wildlife feeding hobby. Since many of our mammal guests are abroad only at night, if we are to see them, we should locate their feeding area in a part of the yard receiving artificial light. The skunks, possums, raccoons and flying squirrels that come to feed will prove to be entertaining guests.

Roza Freundlich from New York states that she puts out old bananas, meat scraps and "anything edible" to feed skunks. Sharon Steinwachs, also in New York, states that whenever there is food on the ground, the squirrels will generally go for it and leave the feeders alone. The same holds true when there is an abundant supply of natural foods. I have noted this where I live; and S. Glenn Utz in Louisiana comments that squirrels visit his feeders only when there has been a poor acorn and nut crop.

SPILLAGE AND WASTE

Regardless of the season, we will want to establish economic feeding practices that allow birds to receive maximum benefits from our offerings. A big step in this direction is to keep more expensive foods off the ground and in feeders that were designed to hold them. This means placing sunflower seeds in sunflower feeders, thistle seeds in thistle feeders, etc. But even if the seeds are in proper feeders, some seed is spilled as birds feed. Unless there is a tray below the feeder, these will fall to the ground. Therefore it is a good idea to buy the small tray that attaches to most tube feeders. On the other hand, little can be done about the messy feeding habits of some birds. Chickadees and nuthatches, for example, toss out or drop many more seeds than they are likely to eat. These seeds will not necessarily be wasted. Mourning doves and other ground-feeding birds can be counted upon to gobble them up.

CLEANING FEEDERS

Something as simple as cleaning feeders every few weeks can make a difference in the feed bill and also protect birds from the dangers of moldy food. Even the best designed present day bird feeders are not proof against contamination by moisture. Condensation of moisture will take place inside the feeder; and rain or snow can enter most feeders by way of feeding ports. Moisture leads to a build-up of bacteria and fungi in the form of molds. Normally birds will reject moldy foods, but if some is eaten along with safe food, they may become ill.

I recall a lady asking me why birds only ate the food in the upper half of her hanging tube-type feeder. The answer was simple. The food in the bottom half of her feeder had become moldy through contamination by moisture. When she removed the bottom of the feeder by taking out two screws, she found the entire bottom half of the feeder filled with a closely packed rotting compost. Naturally she was horrified when she discovered this. Routine cleaning would have prevented such an accumulation.

To prevent contamination from moisture, I bring my hanging tube-type feeders indoors during heavy showers. Also I clean my feeders regularly. First, I disassemble the feeder by undoing screws, and then, using a long-handled brush, I scrub the inside of the tube using warm water and a little detergent. After cleaning the outside, I rinse the entire feeder with clean water and let it dry. The whole operation takes only a few minutes.

THE GROUND FEEDING AREA

The ground below the feeders is subject to the same problems of mold and contamination as the feeders themselves. This is particularly true if the same area is used month after month and year after year for bird feeding. But with proper management, we can safely continue to supply food in the same general area. By far the best practice is to mulch the entire feeding area with a thick layer of wood chips. The chips will act as a filter, draining away water and absorbing hulls, bird droppings and other debris. When the chips start to rot, it is time to remove them and apply another application of chips. Birds love to scratch in the chips, and the whole area begins to look more tidy once we have resorted to this method of landscaping. By using wood chips we make the bird feeding area look like another flower bed. This is one way to beautify the yard!

CHAPTER SEVEN

WATER FOR BATHING AND DRINKING

Watching birds at water is as enjoyable as watching them at bird feeders. Coming to drink, bathe, or both, they exhibit a lack of concern that is rare in wild birds. Their shyness seems to vanish as soon as they begin splashing about in the water.

A cedar waxwing enjoys splashing itself clean.

Although bathing for birds has its practical side, they seem to come to water as much for sheer enjoyment as they do for cleanliness and feather care. Usually they drink first, and then may go on to take one or more baths. Bathing activity usually takes place in spurts. The sight of one bird splashing about in the water seems to touch off a round of bathing by other birds in the immediate vicinity. Amid fluttering of wings and heads ducking under, birds may keep up their vigorous bathing activity for many minutes. One by one, the birds, wet and thoroughly bedraggled, will leave the water and go to nearby shrubbery to preen their feathers. Many will return to the bath for still more rounds of bathing.

As a part of any summer feeding program, water should be used in ways best suited to the needs of our birds while still providing us with good viewing opportunities. Unlike food, we have only one ingredient to deal with — water itself. How to utilize this life-giving substance in ways to best benefit birds has received little attention until recent years.

In the past, the bird bath was primarily a garden ornament. The centerpiece of a formal garden or at the end of a garden path, it lent a certain charm and beauty to the scene. Whether or not it was used by birds seemed to make little difference.

The trend today is to give first consideration to birds. The old-fashioned bird bath is literally being taken down from its pedestal and used in better ways to accommodate birds. Light- weight baths, handsome and easy-to-move, are replacing the ponderous models of the past. The present day bird bath often adds as much to the garden landscape as the older ones did. Moreover, the newer models can be moved easily if we decide they are not in exactly the right places.

THE RIGHT LOCATION

In placing our bird baths, we need first to consider our needs as bird watchers. Through the winter, many of us have been glued behind windows unable to fully enjoy the sounds and sights of nature. As the weather becomes warmer, we begin to spend more and more time on the outdoor balcony, the deck, patio or lawn chair. Our bird baths, like our feeding stations, should be located in parts of the yard easily visible from our new vantage points. The birds will quickly become used to our presence and will go about their activities in the same ways as before.

Another factor in locating our bird baths is presence of a nearby source of water. We are in luck if an outdoor faucet or hose is within reach of the bath. These outlets will permit us to easily fill the bath whenever needed. Sometimes it is possible to keep a small, steady trickle of water running into the bath. Mrs. J. S. Vaughan in Wisconsin has her bird bath below a dripping faucet. On the other hand, Paul Clopper in California uses a system that could well be the envy of anyone supplying water to both plants and birds. He has a drip system on a timer to water the plants while he is gone. One of the lines, he states, runs to the bird bath. This insures that it gets water every day and stays fairly clean.

As in locating bird feeders, we need to find places where there is a fair amount of shade and cover. Although a bird bath doesn't have to be in complete shade, it should be shaded enough so that the water does not become overly warm. But if the bath receives a continuous flow of water from a faucet or some other source, shade is not so important.

Cover is doubly important at a bird bath. After taking a bath, a bird almost inevitably flies to the nearest tree or shrub to begin drying itself and preening its feathers. This is a vital ritual. A bird that is thoroughly wet cannot fly as well and therefore is especially vulnerable to capture by a predator. If no plants are near the site where we have decided to place a bird bath, we can always plant some. Everyday garden shrubs like lilac, forsythia, holly and privet will do nicely.

Gently dripping water draws visitors like this yellow throat and red-eyed vireo.

Should we place the bird bath near a bird feeder? My advice would be close enough so that we can view both from wherever we do our bird watching but not so close that chaff and other debris fall from the feeder into the bath. Normally a separation of four to five feet is an adequate distance. But I prefer a wider separation than this so that we do not confuse feeding station behavior with bird bath behavior. Having the bird bath and bird feeder reasonably near each other does permit birds from both to easily go to the same plants for cover.

This is not to say that we should always hold to this kind of arrangement. Much depends upon how many bird baths and feeders we finally decide upon and how birds respond to the locations where they are placed. It didn't take me long to discover that two bird baths outside my kitchen window were more than were needed at this one location. A single bird bath is adequate for a location on the opposite side of the house. So now I am looking for a good location for one of the two baths I have outside the kitchen window. It will need to be at a place where birds can find it and where it can conveniently be viewed from a window or side porch.

If cats are a problem, the bird bath should be well out in the open, away from places where cats can crouch and lie in wait. We have dogs, and therefore cats are not a problem in our yard. However, in defense of cats, it should be pointed out that many cats do not molest birds. I heard of a tom cat that didn't bother birds but did the birds a service by chasing all other cats out of a yard.

A small drinking dish on a railing proves inviting to a lesser goldfinch.

THE STANDARD BIRD BATH

Although we usually get by with less food and fewer feeders in summer, this is not true with bird baths. Not only do birds need more water in hot, dry weather but convenience is an important factor. It is enough of a hardship for parents, busy with nesting duties, to fly a long distance to obtain water but virtually an impossibility with fledglings barely able to fly. As we learned from our questionnaires, many of our respondents began adding bird baths and offering water in other ways in early summer. Among extra containers used were flower pot saucers, pans, dishes, pie plates, hub caps, garbage can lids and frying pans. Placed on the ground and kept well filled, containers such as these do offer handy sources of water when birds most need it.

Birds also respond well to lawn sprinkler systems. Gathering on the portion of the lawn being sprinkled, they go through the same bathing performances that they do at the bird bath.

But summer or winter, the standard bird bath, whether an old-fashioned one or newer model, is what most of us depend upon. The basic design remains the same — a bowl-shaped basin with sides sloping gradually to the center and the greatest depth no more than 2 to 3 inches. Aside from lighter-weight materials used in construction, the only other major way in which newer baths differ from older ones is *no pedestal*. If anything, birds prefer coming to the ground for water. This is normally where they find it. We need only witness the frenzy of drinking and bathing activity that takes place at roadside puddles to know how attuned birds are to finding their water on the ground. Without its pedestal, the bird bath closely approximates the roadside puddle. This is perhaps the reason why birds come so readily to ground-level bird baths and other water-filled containers on the ground. The bird bath, however, does have a big advantage over the roadside puddle. If properly maintained, it is a permanent fixture; the puddle most likely will soon dry up.

PROPER CARE

Something about a bird bath seems to instill the belief that it needs little if any care. Sandra Parshall in Virginia takes note of this when she says, "it is amazing how many people have bird baths but never fill them or clean them." She goes on to call water more important than food and adds that "anyone can have dozens of beautiful birds in the yard by just putting out a container of clean water."

To clean and refill a bird bath is such a quick and easy chore that it is a wonder more people do not make a habit of doing this. I usually check my bird baths every time I go out to refill the bird feeders. Usually I will need to do nothing more than add some water and remove any leaves or other debris that have fallen into the baths.

Even when the bath is not heavily used, it requires scrubbing and refilling. In summer, any small, partly stagnant body of water soon becomes discolored from tiny aquatic plants known as algae. Forming a scum on the water and coating the sides of improperly cared for bird baths, the algae can become a real menace if we let it get out of hand. To stop the growth of algae and keep the water clean, we should empty bird baths every few days, scrub them, and refill them with fresh water.

Cleaning procedures for concrete baths are different than those for plastic or aluminum baths. A thorough scouring with a stiff wire brush will serve to remove algae and other deposits from a concrete bird bath. With the help of Bon Ami and a nylon brush, similar deposits can be removed from plastic or aluminum baths without scratching the surface. Also Scotch-Brite, the scouring pad, comes in handy for cleaning plastic and aluminum baths. Make sure that all traces of any cleansing powder have been removed before adding water to the bath. I usually use a stiff broom and a hose in the final stages of cleaning my baths.

FLOWING OR DRIPPING WATER

Not many of us are lucky enough to have a bubbling brook flowing through our yards. If we did, we would have an ideal place for birds to drink and bathe. Birds are attracted to moving water more than they are to the quiet water of a pond or lake. The place I used to find goldfinches bathing most frequently was in the ripples of a shallow stream that emptied from a small pond. The flowing water was more attractive to them than the placid waters of the pond.

If we could somehow recirculate the water in our bird bath so that it would pass through a filter and then flow back into the bath, we would be close to offering birds the same rippling water that is found in a small stream. How can this be done without much trouble and expense? The answer is any one of several small, electric pumps sold at garden stores along with filters and tubing. These supplies, commonly used to recycle water in garden fish and lily ponds, can be used in several ways to enhance the beauty and effectiveness of our bird bath operation. As seen in questionnaire returns, some of our respondents created small waterfalls, others fountains, and still others had tiered bird baths. The tiered bath is one in which water flows from an elevated bath down to one somewhat lower, and from this one to a still lower bath. Normally three is the number of baths linked together in a system of this kind and powered by a small electric pump. C. E. Allen, who lives in the Sierra Nevada Range in California, tells of his joy at having bluebirds come to his tiered bird bath. Judging from the location of his home, we suspect his guests were mountain bluebirds, a far western species.

Whether we use bubblers, tricklers, misters, drippers that attach to a regular hose faucet or tiered bird baths, we have accomplished our objective of keeping water in motion. Even a slow drip from a hose hanging from a tree will achieve the same end. Not only will water in motion attract many more birds than still water, but, with any of the systems I have mentioned, the bird bath will *not* go dry.

Although fewer than four per cent of our respondents said they were using water in any of the ways described above, it seems likely that more and more people will catch on. The possibilities are endless. On the other hand, nearly all of our respondents had bird baths of more conventional types. Most people do not need to be told that birds need water in summer.

THE RUSH HOUR

Anyone who has had experience in watching birds at bird baths will know that birds respond to water more readily under some conditions than others. I am sure I am able to pin-point only a few of the reas-

A Bullock's oriole preens and rearranges its feathers after a bath.

ons that bring birds to my baths in greater numbers than usual. Perhaps readers have observed birds coming to water for other reasons than those I mention below.

Some of the busiest rounds of drinking and bathing at my baths have occurred when birds have been eating astringent fruits like wild cherries. To keep flocks of robins and cedar waxwings supplied with water at such times, I have to refill my bird baths many more times than usual. I know what the birds have been eating from the seeds and pits they cough up while they are in the bath.

As might be expected, hot, dry weather brings birds to bird baths in greater numbers than usual. Strangely, though, birds are likely to drink and bathe more than usual in hot weather just before a rain storm, and even for a while after the rain has begun to fall. They do this even when the rain is accompanied by a marked drop in temperature. I have often wondered about this and have tentatively concluded that an approaching storm awakens birds from the lethargy they have been in during hotter parts of the day. Like ourselves, birds conserve their energy on a hot day by becoming less active and seeking out the shade. But when clouds gather and temperatures drop on a hot day, they begin pursuing normal activities again.

Do birds cool themselves by bathing? This is another question connected with bird bath use in hot weather. Unlike us, birds do not perspire. Taking a bath or wetting itself under a garden sprinkler system probably does little to cool a bird's body temperature. A bird's feathers insulate it from all but drastic temperature changes. A bird must drink more than usual if its internal cooling system is to function properly. Panting and vaporization of moisture from the lungs and associated air sacs help prevent birds from getting overly warm in very hot weather. So drink they must when the temperatures climb into the nineties and higher. Mourning doves were found to drink four times as much water at 100 degrees as they did at 70 degrees. This is good reason to keep our bird baths well filled with clean water when the mercury climbs.

DUST BATHING

Still another form of bathing, the dust bath, may be indulged in by birds for the same reasons they take water baths. Relief from itching and feather care may be the chief motives. Among the dust bathers we may see in our yards are the house sparrow, flicker, bobwhite, ring-necked pheasant and wren. The sparrow not only bathes long and vigorously in dust but goes from the dust pile to the bird bath to continue its cleansing. Jeanette Urbain in Washington complains of house sparrows going to the bird bath after dusting themselves and making the water so dirty that other birds wouldn't use it. Fortunately, the problem she mentions does not seem to be very common.

YOUNG AT THE BIRD BATH

The bird bath, like the feeding station, is a wonderful place to watch bird behavior. Young birds recently out of the nest must learn to drink and bathe on their own. They do this by watching older birds.

At first, standing timidly at the edge of the bath, they watch as other birds take to the water. Then gingerly stepping in themselves, after perhaps having first tested the water with their bills and sipped a little, they begin splashing like the other birds. It may take them only one lesson to learn how to drink and bathe. They soon catch on to the routine and visit the bath when other birds do.

They have learned how to drink and bathe much more quickly than they have learned how to feed themselves. This is perhaps because indulgent parents will continue to feed them even when they should be on their own. Have you watched young birds at your bird baths? If not, here is another of summer's treats waiting in store for you.

CHAPTER EIGHT

ATTRACTING HUMMINGBIRDS

O ne of the best things about summer bird feeding is that we have more opportunities to branch out and to explore new ways to feed and attract birds. Hummingbirds offer us just the opportunity we have been waiting for. Who hasn't wanted to see these tiny colorful birds close at hand and become better acquainted with them? Along the East Coast we begin to see hummingbirds as early as March in the South, and April and May farther north. On the other hand, in parts of the West a few are present the year 'round; others, timing their arrivals to the opening of favorite wildflowers, can be expected about the time flowers come into bloom. Flashing bright colors as they make the rounds of the garden, the new arrivals, all too often, are present one day and absent the next. How can we detain them?

Around the turn of the century, a young lady seated outside, while recovering from an illness, made a surprising discovery. Sitting quietly and holding a flower in her hand, she had the satisfaction of having a hummingbird come to the flower and sip nectar. Next she offered a

Rufous hummingbird sits on its nest in a rosebush.

flower of the same kind placed in a container partly filled with a sugar-water solution. On returning, the hummer not only went to the flower but dipped its bill into the solution. Soon the bird was making more visits. This simple experiment showed that hummingbirds in the wild will accept artificial nectar. The whole concept of feeding hummingbirds is based upon this single finding.

It wasn't long before hummingbird feeding became a popular hobby. Instead of closing down feeding operations when the weather became warmer, people now had an incentive to become involved in still another bird feeding activity. The hummers would soon arrive to replace winter birds like juncos and white-throated and white-crowned sparrows that depart northward with the coming of warm spring weather. The tiny birds, with their different habits and different tastes, would require different methods on our part if we were to be successful in attracting them. As stated by Barbara Ramming in Texas, "feeding hummingbirds in the summer is our greatest challenge."

If we succeed in attracting a single hummer to a feeder, chances are we will be in the business of feeding these small birds for years to come. Others will follow the first one to the feeder, and chances are good, that with every subsequent year of supplying food, we will have still more hummers. Mrs. David Gongwer of Ashland, Ohio started out with only two ruby-throated hummingbirds, but by the end of ten years more than one hundred were coming to her feeders. This is many more than most of us in the East ever see in our yards. But westerners, with far more hummingbirds, aren't surprised when their yards are filled with the excitement of a sudden influx which may see four or five species visiting flowers and feeders. When this happens, as it sometimes does during the migration period, the remedy is to put out more feeders and make more solution. One year, Mrs. Will Williams of Granite Station, California had as many as 45 feeders in use and was offering over 4 gallons of sugar-water solution a day during the peak of late summer migration. Mrs. Kenneth Hughes in Idaho tells us her hummers drink 5 to 6 quarts of syrup daily for a period of about 3 weeks in summer. When wild honey-suckle comes into bloom, they largely desert her feeders and feed upon natural nectar.

For those who have not yet had their first visit from a hummer, the sound of hundreds at one time may seem like an impossibility. But the best advice is *do not give up*. Sandra S. Riddle of Anderson, South Carolina said she tried for five years to attract hummers to feeders without success. Then she discovered that by tying red ribbons that would flutter in the wind to her feeders, the birds took notice and started using them. Once a feeder was discovered, the ribbon was no longer needed.

Ruby-throated hummingbirds put on an aerial show at the feeder outside the window.

HOW MANY KINDS AND
WHERE THEY COME FROM

The hummingbirds make up a strictly New World family composed of some 341 species. Their homeland is the American tropics stretching from Mexico to Peru and Brazil. For the most part, those that reach our latitude have migrated northward from the tropics. They arrive in spring, nest and return to their tropical home in late summer and early fall. The ruby-throated hummingbird, the only species to nest east of the Mississippi, flies across the wide expanse of the Gulf of Mexico on its migrations. The rufous hummingbird, a far western species with a breeding range from California to Alaska, makes a round trip of as much as 4,000 miles each year. Out West there are sixteen breeding species and a number of others that wander northward from Mexico.

HOW TO ATTRACT

Curious over anything that is brightly colored and given to probing unfamiliar objects with their long bills, hummers can often be attracted to feeders in the way suggested by Sandra. Red, more than any other color, excites their curiosity. This is why red is so often used to lure hummingbirds to bird feeders. Whether we use a red ribbon, red crepe paper or a feeder that has some red on it, any hummingbird in the vicinity will almost certainly zoom in to investigate.

We should also have a good display of red flowers in our yard or in window boxes. Red flowers are the best advertisement we can give hummers as they return north in the spring. Red-flowered hibiscus, geraniums, fuchsias, garden balsams, petunias, salvias and begonias make excellent lures. This is particularly true if we display the plants when little else is in bloom. The proper time to begin luring hummers with blossoms and feeders is a few days before the first spring migrants arrive in your area.

Feeders should be placed where they are easily visible to both the hummingbirds and us. Once discovered, a hummingbird feeder stands a good chance of being patronized for the rest of the season. Moreover,

First attracted by flowers, this Anna's hummingbird soon moves on to the feeder.

hummingbirds have such good memories that the following spring former patrons begin searching the exact locations where feeders once hung.

SUGAR NOT HONEY

Sugar is the proper ingredient to use in preparing a solution to go into feeders. It should be granulated, white table sugar, the kind we are all familiar with. Like nectar, white sugar supplies the quick energy so vital to the existence of these overly active birds. Hummingbirds have faster heartbeats, faster breathing rates and higher body temperatures than any other kinds of birds. They must eat frequently and eat a lot. The late Dr. Augusto Ruschi, noted Brazilian authority on hummingbirds, stated that some species consume 30 times their own weight in food a day!

The matter of how much sugar to use in preparing our solution has long been debated. In a 1960 issue of *Audubon Magazine*, John K. Terres pointed out that a 1 part sugar to 2 parts water solution fed to captive hummingbirds in the New York Zoological Gardens was harmful to them and could lead to liver damage. Today the recommended solution is 1 part sugar to 4 parts water. This strength closely approximates the sucrose or sugar content of nectar in flowers.

Well-intentioned efforts to provide hummingbirds with a food more nutritious than white sugar have generally led to failure. For a time a mixture of honey and water was recommended as superior over sugar and water. But in 1949, Dr. Ruschi warned that a honey solution could produce a fatal fungus disease in hummers effecting their tongues. The findings of Dr. Ruschi were corroborated by Jan Roger van Oosten of Seattle, Washington who found that his captive hummers died when they were fed a honey- water solution.

To obtain the 1 part sugar to 4 parts water mixture use 1 tablespoon of sugar to 1/4 cup of water, or 1/4 cup of sugar to 1 cup of water. Barely bring the water to a boil, add the sugar and immediately remove the container from the stove. Allow the solution to cool before replenishing feeders. Any left-over solution should be kept in a refrigerator.

SAFETY PRECAUTIONS

It is a common practice to add a small amount of red food coloring to the solution before filling feeders. This is done both to lure hummingbirds to the feeder and to help us determine the amount of fluid left in the feeder. We can see a red mixture better than a colorless one. Red food dyes have, however, come under suspicion as being carcinogenic. Many feel the red coloring is perhaps unsafe and also unnecessary. If the feeder is not already red or partly red, we can use red tape or red nail polish on surfaces of feeding ports as an alternative form of advertisement.

An equally worrisome concern is black mold forming in the feeder solution. Primarily a hot weather problem, mold is apt to develop if hummers are not drinking the solution fast enough. Any solution that has been left in feeders three days or more in hot weather soon becomes cloudy. We will see black specks in the liquid and mold beginning to form on the inside surface of the glass or plastic reservoir of the feeder. We can solve the mold problem by changing the solution before it has a chance to form. Always rinse the feeder in warm water before adding fresh solution. If we are too late and mold has already begun to form, add vinegar to the rinse and also grains of uncooked rice. Shake vigorously, empty, rinse again using warm water; then add fresh solution. In stubborn cases use a small stiff brush with a flexible wire handle to get at deposits. Tiny percolator brushes are ideal for getting into crevices.

The problem of mold can easily be overcome with extra attention to cleaning and by using only the amount of solution that will be quickly consumed by hummers. As stated by Mrs. George W. Proctor in Utah, "you have to keep hummingbird feeders clean. I fill mine several times a day."

ANT, BEE, AND WASP PROBLEMS

The sugar-water sipped by hummingbirds is also well-liked by many insect species. So long as the insects appear infrequently and in small numbers, there is nothing for us to worry about. Big incursions of ants and swarms of bees are another matter. I find ants easier to cope with than bees and other stinging insects. As a rule, all I have to do is smear liberal amounts of petroleum jelly (Vaseline) on the wire or metal rod to which the feeder is attached. Repeat the application as soon as ants begin to crawl over the jelly. Moving the feeder to another location is sometimes an effective way to cope with an ant problem.

Petroleum jelly, as well as salad oil, is useful in combatting bees and their close relatives. This time, smear the ingredient on surfaces immediately adjacent to feeding vents. Use only a little and repeat applications for as long as a problem exists. Treatment with oil or jelly makes the surface unsuitable for landing by bees, hornets and wasps. Bee guards, supplied with many makes of feeders, help but can't always be depended upon.

OTHER BIRDS AT FEEDERS

To the joy of some and misgivings of others, birds other than hummingbirds also like sugar-water and visit feeders to get their share. The main complaint is that these extra guests take more than their share.

Anne Freeman-Gallimore in New Mexico asks for advice on how to keep house finches from using hummingbird feeders. She states that they learned how to drink from three different kinds of feeders and taught their friends. Bribery is the only solution I know of in coping with this problem. For example, Sally Hoyt Spofford, who feeds hummingbirds the year 'round at Portal, Arizona, provides easy-to-drink-from open cups filled with sugar- water for the house finches, orioles, tanagers and other birds that offer competition at hummingbird feeders. The other birds go to these cups instead of fluttering before hummingbird feeders.

The same open cups are visited at night by small mammals. Among these nocturnal visitors are raccoons, foxes, coatimundis and ringtails (members of the cat family). Mrs. Spofford and her husband feel

Sugar-water also attracts fascinating night visitors like raccoons, and in the West, ringtails.

an obligation to feed whatever wildlife comes their way, regardless of whether these visitors are a nuisance. Many of those who feed hummingbirds have the same philosophy as the Spoffords. They don't mind providing extra food for other guests and often take delight in adding new species to the feeding station list. The appeal of sugar-water to birds seems to lie in the fact that it is thirst-quenching and sweet. Like ourselves, birds enjoy anything sweet.

Pat Murphy and I, when doing a hummingbird article for a 1985 issue of *Bird Watcher's Digest*, compiled a list of 56 avian species, other than hummingbirds, noted at hummingbird feeders. In California, besides ubiquitous house finches, the feeders attracted such birds as hooded and northern orioles, chestnut-backed chickadees, plain titmice and ruby-crowned kinglets. Hummingbird feeders in a yard in Tucson, Arizona attracted Gila woodpecker, flicker, orioles including Scott's oriole, orange-crowned warbler and verdin. A Vermont hummingbird feeder attracted the sapsucker, hairy and downy woodpeckers, and a black-throated blue warbler.

For those interested in attracting a wide variety of birds to their yards, hummingbird feeders have a special place. They often lure birds we might not get at feeders offering other foods.

FEEDERS

Choosing a hummingbird feeder is not always easy. We should start off, if possible, with a reliable model that is free of defects and which is well suited to the needs of our hummingbird guests. I insist upon a feeder that is easy-to-clean, easy-to- fill and easy for hummers to use. In addition, I want the feeder to be durable enough to last for years.

In hot weather, particularly if the feeder is exposed to the sun, the air column inside the reservoir holding the syrup expands causing the feeder to drip. Some designs are more prone to dripping than others. It does help to keep feeders in the shade during hot weather.

Pet store water bottles for guinea pigs, hamsters and cage birds can be used as hummingbird feeders. Improvised feeders, such as these, are useful in luring hummingbirds and telling us where we should place better, more permanent models.

WHEN TO STOP FEEDING

People were formerly advised to stop feeding hummers as soon as fall migration got underway. It was believed the presence of an unlimited food supply would cause birds to delay their departure or cause some of them not to migrate at all. These worries are unfounded. Inner promptings tell birds when to migrate. Most birds, including hummingbirds, depart southward in the fall when their favorite foods are in peak supply. We do, however, sometimes see one or more birds that have failed to migrate. Their presence is due to some type of physical or psychological impairment and not anything we have done.

It is true that along the west coast and border states with Mexico certain species of hummingbirds have always spent, or are now beginning to spend, the winter with us. The outstanding example is Anna's hummingbird, a west coast species that now winters as far north as Washington and southwestern British Columbia. Without help from sugar-water feeders, it is doubtful if these northern residents could get through the winter. Although small flying insects appear on warmer days and there is other food such as sap oozing from trees, the winter hummingbird is hard pressed if we discontinue offering food. During cold spells, we may need to attach a light bulb next to the feeder to keep the solution from freezing. Fresh supplies can be offered when older ones freeze.

For most of us, however, such precautions are not needed. By far the greatest number of hummers leave us in the fall, and we do not see them again until sometime in spring. If no hummers have come to your feeders for a week, it is safe to take them down. The one thing to avoid is taking the feeders down when birds are still present.

CHAPTER NINE

CREATING A BACKYARD HABITAT

Having done everything we should in the way of providing food and water, it is appropriate to ask if there is anything else we need to attend to. Judging from a few disappointments reported by our respondents, not everyone is satisfied with the kinds and numbers of birds in yards and at feeding stations. H. Marie Cole in the state of Washington says she would be happy to be able to attract almost any kinds of birds besides the house sparrows and house finches she already has. Sarah Lena Roth in Missouri has only cardinals at her feeders in summer and would like to have titmice and chickadees. Charles A. Mead in Massachusetts says he would love to see bluebirds and cedar waxwings and hear cuckoos. Rachael E. Tupper in Iowa and A. Mayotte in Massachusetts state they once had goldfinches and now no longer have them.

To go into all the reasons birds may be poorly represented or absent in anyone's yard is much beyond the scope of this book. Sometimes it may be a poor nesting season, a delay in the arrival of spring or fall migrants, or simply so much natural food in the wild that there is no incentive for birds to come near us. With reasons such as these, normally all we have to do is wait. Sooner or later birds will put in an appearance. At the same time, it may be that our yard isn't as inviting to birds as it should be. Is it too open, too noisy, too filled with pets, or too closed-in by buildings? Whatever the problem may be, almost always there are steps we can take to make our yard more attractive to birds.

PLANTS

A large yard of several acres or more will almost always have plants that will be attractive to some form of bird life. Even if the yard consists largely of lawn, we can expect good numbers of lawn-feeders. These will include killdeers, mourning doves, robins, starlings, certain of the blackbirds, and goldfinches when dandelions go to seed. The few trees may serve as observation posts for kestrels and bluebirds. The large open yard, however, can be greatly improved upon for birdlife and other wildlife through added plantings. Some might be for shelter, some for nesting sites, some for food. Indeed, most plants serve bird life in a variety of ways.

As I stated in my book *The Wildlife Gardener*, most yards have relatively extensive lawns and not enough space devoted to trees, shrubs, hedges and flower beds. I urge that at least half of our acreage should be in plantings of some kind. I point out that "edge effect," where taller plantings meet openings, is the key to a large and thriving bird population. It is along sunlit edges that birds build their nests and attend to most of their activities. Compared to edge, the interior of a woodland is relatively free of birds.

Another point I stress is proper balance between evergreens and deciduous trees and shrubs. I suggest that about 25 per cent of our woody plantings consist of evergreens, such as pines and hemlocks, and the rest be made up of oaks, maples and others that lose their leaves when cold weather arrives. Evergreens serve as nest sites for some birds and also as shelter and windbreaks. Deciduous plants, on the whole, are better food producers, and they, too, provide nesting sites.

Low plants, such as annuals and perennials, should face lawns and other open spaces, and progressively taller plants should be behind them. I advocate this arrangement of borders and "islands" of taller growth as partial replacement for some of the lawn area. The importance of having a few large trees can scarcely be over-emphasized. As places for orioles to hang their nests and woodland birds to find their food, trees such as elms, maples, oaks, cottonwoods and birches are a "must" if we have room for them. But smaller trees can be equally useful. In *The Wildlife Gardener*, I praise the old apple tree for its many contributions to wildlife. This tree provides birds with food in the form of buds, blossoms and the apples themselves. Even the sap is a relished food. Sapsuckers drill neat little holes through the bark to get at the tasty sap. Other birds, coming to these holes after them, easily enjoy the liquid refreshment as well. Cavities found in many old apple trees provide dens for small mammals and nest holes for cavity-nesting birds.

In spring, a yellow-bellied sapsucker drills holes in trees to feed on the sap.

THE SMALL YARD

Proving small yards can provide as much color and excitement as larger ones, Gustav A. Swanson, with help from a landscape architect, turned an almost bare one-tenth of an acre lot at a home in Fort Collins, Colorado into a bird mecca. Telling of his experience in the 1987 winter issue of *Birder's World*, he offers advice to help all of us make a better garden for birds. Plantings were arranged in such a way that they surrounded three sides of an open area containing bird feeders and a garden pool. The window where the Swansons did most of their viewing looked out on this area. The birds also had their place to view the scene around them — a dead tree planted in the middle of the feeding area. Plantings — some offering food for birds in summer, others offering food at other times of the year — consisted of a wide variety of trees and shrubs. Planted areas were covered with a six-inch layer of wood chips. Of the more than 100 trees and shrubs planted, only one did not survive.

Three years after the plantings had been installed, the Swansons had recorded no fewer than 88 bird species in their small yard. Among their feeding station guests were American goldfinches, white-crowned sparrows, house finches, purple finches, and such distinctively western birds as lazuli buntings, lesser goldfinches and Cassin's finches. What an exciting combination, and imagine finding all these birds, and many others as well, in a small yard in an urban setting!

FOOD PLANTS FOR BIRDS IN SUMMER

The Swansons, like most of us, look forward to having a variety of bright fruits and berries that will serve as ornament as well as food for birds in fall and winter. That is why we usually reserve a large share of our yards for plants such as pyracantha, nandina, flowering crabs, hawthorns, barberries and cotoneasters. The same plants brighten our yard with their flowers in spring and summer; also they serve as cover and nesting sites for birds. But if we are looking for plants that offer birds fruits and berries in summer, we are somewhat limited in our choices. This is especially true in early summer. Even the most persistent fruits that have clung to plants through the winter and spring are gone. To take their place, we do have early fruiting members of the elaeagnus group, such as thorny elaeagnus, and also Nanking cherry, Oregon grape, laurestinus (one of the viburnums) and, if we are willing to put up with the mess that both the tree and the birds leave, white mulberry.

In late summer we have a wider choice. There are more kinds of elaeagnus, cherries and viburnums coming into fruit; also bush honeysuckles, elderberries, blackberries, raspberries, early fruiting dogwood and again, if we don't mind the mess, red mulberry. The latter has a longer fruiting season than white mulberry and, like all mulberries, is tremendously popular with birds. If you have mulberries and cherries with ripe fruit, birds will desert your berry patches, or so it is claimed!

Not to be overlooked in our garden plan are plants that attract hummingbirds. As I note in chapter 8, flowers that invite hummingbirds are typically red, tubular and filled with nectar. We have a wide number to choose from. In *The Wildlife Gardener*, I list some 80 plants recommended as food plants for hummers. Many are handsome ornamentals. Some of the hummingbird plants are vines and others can be grown in flower beds or windowboxes. Therefore, we can have a good display without using much space. This is something to remember if you have a small yard.

Humans think of thistles as weeds, but goldfinches find them a gourmet food.

As I have noted, several of our respondents complained about absence of goldfinches. The reason may have partly been lack of plants on which they feed. If our yard is too neat and tidy without waste areas where dandelions, chicory, thistle and evening primrose can grow, we may not be offering goldfinches enough of an inducement to stay and nest. Goldfinches are known for their habit of not nesting until late summer. They delay nesting because late summer is the time of the year when flowers of the kinds mentioned go to seed. The seeds provide the extra food goldfinches need during their nesting season. By planting such garden flowers as cornflower, cosmos, sweet rocket, marigold and zinnia, we can help hold on to the goldfinches that may have been with us earlier in the summer.

More houses in recent years have reversed the decline of the eastern bluebird.

This not to say we can keep goldfinches in our yards the year 'round even with the help of bird feeders and plants that offer them food. Their migratory habits are such that the birds we see in winter may not be the same ones we see in summer. Like pine siskins, they have a way of suddenly departing even when food is plentiful.

NESTING BOXES

Still another way to invite birds to our yard is to provide nesting sites. This can be done with nesting shelves for birds like robins and boxes or birdhouses for cavity-nesters such as chickadees, titmice, many of the woodpeckers, nuthatches, swallows, wrens and bluebirds. Unfortunately, the two most aggressive cavity-nesters — the house sparrow and European starling — may well frustrate our attempts to provide housing for better liked birds. For this reason, I would suggest careful study and preparation go into any housing program for birds that we may be contemplating. If we are planning houses for bluebirds — one of the most hard-pressed of the cavity-nesters — I would first consult the North American Bluebird Society, Box 6295, Silver Spring, Maryland 20906 and obtain their literature and plans for houses. Marvelous work has been done in providing houses for bluebirds on bluebird trails covering thousands of miles in the states and provinces. But, generally little success can be had in attracting bluebirds to houses in towns and cities. This environment has been taken over by house sparrows and starlings.

As a rule, we will have much better success in luring purple martins to houses in urban or semi-urban areas. These large graceful swallows have become so dependent upon man-made housing that almost everywhere, except in the far West, they have forsaken natural cavities. As with bluebirds, there are special rules to follow in establishing housing for martins. I would suggest consulting The Nature Society, Griggsville, Illinois 62340 for literature on attracting purple martins. Since purple martins live in colonies, multi-chambered houses placed on poles can accommodate a sizable number of nesting pairs.

Ruth Horcher, one of our Florida participants, in only her second year of providing housing for purple martins, states she has no insect problems in her garden nor is she being bitten by insects while the martins are present. Endorsements such as this one make most of us wish we had nesting martins in our yard. But purple martins can be quite choosy about where they will nest. They seem to like the presence of people but need a fair amount of open space in which to conduct their aerial maneuvers.

If we have been defeated in our efforts to supply housing for blue-birds or purple martins, we always have less demanding guests in the form of wrens to fall back upon. Friendly birds that adapt well to man-made environments, wrens will stuff almost any cavity full of sticks and then choose one for nesting purposes. House wrens and Bewick's wrens can squeeze through holes only one inch in diameter and therefore will use birdhouses with entrances small enough to keep out house sparrows and, of course, the much larger starling. Carolina wrens will nest on ledges in out- buildings and sometimes even invade the house itself if they can get in. Cactus wrens nesting in the West are equally fond of sites of this kind. William A. Davis in Tucson, Arizona had cactus wrens nest-ing in his purple martin house and martins nesting in woodpecker cavities in the saguaro cactus in his yard!

A good rule to follow is do not put up birdhouses unless you have certain species in mind you want to accommodate and are willing to inspect your houses frequently. Through inspection or monitoring you see to it that unwanted tenants, from wasps to starlings, have not taken over and everything is going well with the rightful tenants.

NESTING MATERIAL

One of the easiest ways of helping birds during the nesting season is to supply materials they can use in building their nests. If we offer nothing more than pieces of string or yarn cut into short lengths, we will have provided a service we may not know about until leaves are off the trees and we can begin finding bird nests more easily. Easiest to spot are the pendant nests of the northern oriole which are typically fastened to outer branches of elms and other large trees. Irene Lindl in Minnesota supplies twine, yarn, string and pieces of long dry grass as nesting material for orioles and other birds. Jean Bancroft, noting the northern oriole's preference for white nesting material, supplies six-inch lengths of white string and yarn. Orioles leaving the feeding station, where she provides halved oranges, are often seen picking up the nesting material and flying off with it to nests that are under construction. After the young have fledged, they follow the parents to feeders. Mrs. Bancroft says she follows the entire nesting season as she watches the orioles getting nesting material and later returning with the young.

Offering a nesting platform and nesting material will encourage robins to nest.

Mrs. Bancroft also tells us birds in her yard responded readily to strips of Kleenex she put out as nesting material. Kleenex users included the eastern kingbird, willow flycatcher, robin and yellow warbler. A wood thrush nest constructed almost entirely of paper napkins and facial tissues was reported by Hal Harrison in his guide to birds' nests. Other examples of man-made materials in bird nests are given in John K. Terres' *Encyclopedia of North American Birds*. He tells of a warbling vireo's nest made entirely of Kleenex and canyon wren's nest made of paper clips, rubber bands and other office supplies. It has been my observation that nearly every robin's nest in my area contains white paper, cellophane or soft tissue of some kind. Observations such as these suggest that some of the objects we throw out in our trash might be saved as potential nesting material for birds.

Not to be overlooked when the nesting season arrives is something that may be in short supply — a source of sticky, gummy mud that birds can use in nest construction. Among the birds that build their nests partly or wholly of mud are cliff swallows, barn swallows, phoebes, robins, grackles and other blackbirds. In days gone by, birds could always find a good supply of mud around cattle or horse watering troughs. We can come to the rescue by establishing a place in our yard where we moisten the soil enough to create a mud supply.

END OF THE SEASON

If there is any time of the year when it is safe for us to relax and not give as much attention to bird feeders, nest boxes and little extras such as I have mentioned, it is late summer at the end of the nesting season. By mid-August, in most parts of the country, young will be on the wing and, together with parents, getting ready either for a lengthy migration or local wandering. It is at this stage that fully adult birds are beginning to undergo what is known as the postnuptial molt. This is a crucial period when old feathers are shed and new ones grow out to replace them. The molt is a gradual process which sees birds still with their feathers but often looking bedraggled. One can only guess that a bird in molt is experiencing considerable discomfort. Molting birds seem listless and quiet. From late August well into September and even October, our yard is no longer a scene of intense activity.

By now the nesting season is over for most birds except a few late nesters. We can check our birdhouses for the last time and perhaps take some of them down. Old nests should be removed. This is a good time to give our bird feeders a thorough cleaning. I keep right on supplying food so as not to lose the patronage of residents that have been with me all summer. But as soon as the hummingbirds disappear, I take down the sugar-water feeders. Chances are attendance at other feeders will have fallen off. If so, this means putting out less food and perhaps getting by with one or two fewer feeders.

But water, if anything, may be in even more demand during the molting period. By splashing about in water, birds seem able to ease some of the skin discomfort they experience as feathers are lost and new ones begin to grow. A strange performance, known as anting, is seen more often at this time of the year. A bird will either squat in a nest of ants or take ants in its bill and rub them through its plumage. The stings of the ants and the burning sensation that comes from formic acid in the bodies of some ants may actually soothe a bird's irritated skin. Whatever the case may be, we sometimes see birds in odd postures on our lawn and twisting about to reach under the feathers with their bills. The birds may be anting.

As the pace slows down in late summer, we need to remember that it won't be long before birds from regions to the north of us will be arriving. Some of them, bound for regions south of us, may stop by for only a day or two. Others will stay with us through the winter. Offering hospitality to our new guests will be the next item on our agenda. Having feeders already up and filled will make this task easier. Bird baths should also be clean and well filled. A special enticement for many of the newcomers will be the fruits and berries we have in our plantings. If we have a well-rounded program ready and waiting, the fall and winter will be just as rewarding for us as the summer has been.

Planting mulberries will ensure a natural food supply for mockingbirds and others.

The advantages of having a well-rounded bird attracting program is seen in the comments of some of our respondents. Elizabeth Doyle in Michigan writes: "We attract many more birds by providing niches, habitats, water and natural food sources such as flowering fruit and seed producing trees, shrubs and flowers. Augmenting this with feeders in summer assures that birds 'come close' and provide us with a huge, rich reward." Echoing Elizabeth's comments are those of Diane Lea Gett in Connecticut who writes, "As a registered nurse who works in a critical care unit all day, I find attracting birds throughout the year a pleasure. It reduces my stress! I attract birds not only with artificial food but with the trees, shrubs and flowers that I have planted."

CHAPTER TEN

"BIRDS KNOW WHERE TO COME"

O f all the quotes I've given in this book, the one I like best is "the birds know where to come." This one, as we've seen, was supplied by Mildred C. Pokorny in Idaho who had no birds at all at her feeders until she started providing food on a year 'round basis. Once birds became aware of a steady source, they began patronizing her feeders in good numbers.

This past year, I witnessed an example of birds knowing where to come. Through the fall and into early January, attendance was way off at my bird feeders. There were many fewer birds than during the summer months. I attributed this to unusually mild weather and plentiful supplies of natural food. I was not entirely satisfied with this conclusion since I saw few birds in the nearby countryside.

But on January 7th, with heavy skies and falling temperature, I suddenly became aware of more birdlife than I had seen for months. Driving back roads, I saw many flocks of small sparrows, juncos, robins and blackbirds boldly coming to roadsides and entering peoples' yards. Judging from the nervous way the birds moved from one feeding place to another, they were driven by a foreboding or anxiety that I also felt as the bad weather began to close in. That night four to five inches of snow fell. By early morning the falling snow had changed to freezing rain. Soon branches of trees were coated with ice, and roads had become too slippery for safe driving. A major storm was moving up the coast from the south.

The morning of the 8th, my feeders were inundated with birds. The house finches, which had been making only token visits, were landing on top of each other as they scrambled for a place at feeding ports. Whenever there was an opening large enough for another bird to squeeze through, a tufted titmouse or chickadee flew in to seize a sunflower seed and fly off with it. If anything, the activity at small hanging feeders was surpassed by sheer bedlam among a growing flock of common grackles that crowded about below the feeders. Not finding enough food on the ice-covered snow to satisfy their appetites, the grackles began flying up to the hanging feeders. Some of them would precariously balance upon small perches and drive their beaks into feeding ports. Others, too heavy and too ungainly to keep it up for long, would flutter before feeding ports in hummingbird fashion. Not long after the grackles had put in an appearance, cowbirds and red-winged blackbirds arrived. So far as I had been aware, not a single individual among the three blackbird species I've mentioned had appeared at my feeders that fall or in December. Yet the birds knew that my yard was a place to come during an emergency.

Viewing the seething mass of birdlife in my yard from my windows, I realized I would have to do something soon if I were to prevent the hordes of blackbirds from usurping the entire feeding area. My first move was to empty a large container of cracked corn on the icy surface of what had been my lawn. Used to lesser fare and perhaps as fond of it as of sunflower seeds, the blackbirds swarmed to the corn and temporarily left my feeders to the smaller birds. I won't say the battle had been won; I would have to devise still other strategies. Although it took several days of experimenting, I did finally achieve what might be called a *modus vivendi*.

I removed my offering of sunflower seed and substituted thistle and safflower seed instead. Only under emergency conditions will grackles and other blackbirds touch such fare. Although the blackbirds would gingerly eat seeds that had fallen from thistle or safflower feeders, they no longer performed impossible acrobatic feats to eat at the feeders. Furthermore, I put in service several anti-blue jay feeders that I had in reserve. These feeders have flexible, spring perches that give way if a large bird alights on them but which will hold a bird the size of a house finch. Once a grackle had an unpleasant experience at one of these perches, it did not come back.

It wasn't long before cardinals, white-throats, juncos, goldfinches and house finches were eating happily at the feeders, and the grackles, in much fewer numbers than before, hovered disconsolately at the edge of the feeding area. When, after a week, the harsh weather began to moderate, the grackles and other blackbirds disappeared; they have not been back.

I learned two lessons from this episode. One was that birds, even when they appear to be scarce or absent, are lingering somewhere. They know about us and our food and will come streaming in when there is an emergency. The other lesson was that, with a change in menu and the use of more selective bird feeders, we can limit the impact of a sudden influx of birds that otherwise would dominate the feeders. The measures I used with grackles and other blackbirds can be applied with equal success to other large, aggressive birds and will work equally well in winter or summer. So whether the problem species is a grackle, blue jay, scrub jay, pigeon or mourning dove, there are solutions available. Also it is well to remember that sudden incursions of the kind I have mentioned are generally temporary in nature. Very often all we have to do is wait for a change in the weather and the birds will go away. Grackles, for example, do not like us any more than we like them. They would much rather be feeding in open fields.

There are many more positive sides to feeding birds than negative ones. For a quick review of the ground I have covered in this book, I have listed the following:

1. The extra food at the feeding station helps insure nesting success and reduces hazards to parent birds.
2. Generally, there are fewer birds at feeders in summer than there are in winter.
3. People have closer contacts with birds in summer because they spend more time out-of-doors.
4. By attracting more birds to the yard, feeders exert an influence in reducing the effects of an insect outbreak.
5. Birds are not diverted from eating insects by having food available at bird feeders. Insects take first priority.
6. The feeding station is a good place to observe courtship behavior and other behavior related to the nesting season.

7. Feeding stations offer good opportunities for us to see parents feeding young.

8. Only under exceptional circumstances should we try to rescue a young bird out of the nest and unable to fly.

9. Black oil sunflower seeds are especially recommended for summer bird feeding.

10. Other good foods to offer include thistle seeds, safflower seeds, suet and suet mixes, fruits and water-softened raisins.

11. Water is almost as important as food in summer and is more enticing to birds if it is in motion.

12. Special care should be given to cleaning bird baths and keeping them properly filled.

13. Hummingbird feeding is a whole other side to summer bird feeding and can be very rewarding. But special care should be given to the sugar solution and cleanliness to combat mold.

14. Suitable plantings greatly enhance a yard's attractiveness to birds. Plants should be chosen from the standpoint of food, nesting sites and cover.

15. The placing of nesting boxes should not be undertaken unless we have certain cavity-nesting species in mind and tailor our program to the needs of these species. Boxes should be monitored at intervals after they are placed.

16. Supplying nesting material is an easy and useful way to help birds during the nesting season.

17 Feeding and caring for birds in summer, or at any season, help people almost as much as they help birds.

Summer bird feeding allows us to know this mountain chickadee in a special way.

BIRDS TO LOOK FOR AND ENJOY AT FEEDERS IN SUMMER FOODS AND REGIONS WHERE FOUND IN SUMMER

DUCKS

Two species, easy to attract: bread, corn, other grains

Wood duck—east and far west
Mallard—widespread

FOWL-LIKE BIRDS

Three species, easy to attract in suitable habitat: seeds and grain, especially corn

Northern bobwhite—eastern
California quail—far west
Ring-necked pheasant—widespread, northern states

PIGEONS AND DOVES

Three species: seeds, grain, bakery products

Band-tailed pigeon—western
Domestic pigeon (unpopular at feeders)—widespread
Mourning dove—widespread

GREATER ROADRUNNER

One species (southwest): sometimes responds to small pieces of raw meat tossed its way

HUMMINGBIRDS

Eight species common at feeders: sugar/water
(1 part sugar to 4 parts water)

Ruby-throated hummingbird—eastern
Broad-tailed hummingbird—western
Calliope hummingbird—far western
Anna's hummingbird—far western
Black-chinned hummingbird—western
Costa's hummingbird—far southwest
Rufous hummingbird—far western
Allen's hummingbird—far western

WOODPECKERS

Seven species, most of them common at feeders: suet, fresh fruit, sometimes sunflower, peanuts and other seeds

Northern flicker—widespread
Pileated woodpecker (rare visitor)—widespread
Red-bellied woodpecker—eastern
Red-headed woodpecker—eastern and plain's states
Acorn woodpecker—far western
Hairy woodpecker—widespread
Downy woodpecker—widespread

JAYS

Five species, first three easy to attract: suet, sunflower, nutmeats

Blue jay—widespread
Steller's jay—western
Scrub jay—western
Pinyon jay—western
Gray jay—mountains in west and northern

BLACK-BILLED MAGPIE

One species (western), uncommon at feeders and potentially a nuisance: meat and other scraps

CLARK'S NUTCRACKER

One species (western), not uncommon at feeders in mountains: suet, meat and other scraps

AMERICAN CROW

One species (widespread), unpopular at feeders: suet, meat and other scraps

CHICKADEES AND TITMICE

Six species, all highly receptive to foods at feeders: sunflower, safflower, suet

Black-capped chickadee—widespread
Carolina chickadee—southeast
Mountain chickadee—mountain areas of the West
Chestnut-backed chickadee—far western
Tufted titmouse—eastern
Plain titmouse—western

BUSHTIT

One species (western), difficult to attract: suet

NUTHATCHES

Four species, first two highly receptive to foods at feeders: sunflower, suet, nutmeats

White-breasted nuthatch—widespread
Red-breasted nuthatch—widespread northern and mountains
Brown-headed nuthatch—southeast
Pygmy nuthatch—western

WRENS

Three species, for the most part hard to attract in summer: suet, nutmeats, raw hamburger

House wren—widespread
Bewick's wren—south-central and western
Carolina wren—eastern

MOCKINGBIRD AND THRASHERS

Three species, not easy to attract without special foods: softened raisins, fresh fruit, bakery products

Northern mockingbird—widespread
Gray catbird—widespread, but chiefly eastern
Brown thrasher-widespread, but chiefly eastern

ROBIN AND BLUEBIRDS

Three species, robin more easily attracted than bluebirds: softened raisins, fresh fruit, bakery products

American robin—widespread
Eastern bluebird—eastern
Western bluebird—western

CEDAR WAXWING

One species, hard to attract: softened raisins, currants, apples

EUROPEAN STARLING

One species (widespread), unpopular at feeders and primarily attracted to soft foods: suet, kitchen scraps, small seeds (not sunflower, thistle, or safflower)

WARBLERS

Three species, seldom visit feeders: suet, finely crushed nutmeats, bakery products

Yellow warbler—widespread
Pine warbler—eastern
American redstart—widespread

HOUSE SPARROW

One species (widespread), unpopular at feeders: cracked corn, mixed birdseed, bakery products

MEADOWLARKS

Two species, hard to attract to feeders: corn, wheat, mixed birdseed

Eastern meadowlark—eastern
Western meadowlark—western

BLACKBIRDS, GRACKLE, AND COWBIRD

Five species, for the most part unpopular at feeders: sunflower, mixed birdseed, corn and other grain, bakery products

Red-winged blackbird—widespread
Brewer's blackbird—widespread, chiefly western
Rusty blackbird—eastern
Common grackle—widespread, chiefly eastern
Brown-headed cowbird—widespread

ORIOLES

Four species, not always easy to attract: sugar/water, softened raisins, fresh fruit

Orchard oriole—eastern
Scott's oriole—southwest
Hooded oriole—southwest
Northern oriole—widespread (an eastern and a western race)

TANAGERS

Three species, difficult to attract: sugar/water, fresh fruit, suet

Western tanager—western
Scarlet tanager—eastern
Summer tanager—widespread in more southern states

CARDINAL AND PYRRHULOXIA

Two species, the first is easy to attract and common at bird feeders: sunflower, safflower, cracked corn, mixed birdseed

Northern cardinal—widespread chiefly eastern
Pyrrhuloxia—southwest

GROSBEAKS

Four species, the first three come readily to bird feeders: sunflower, safflower, melon seeds

Rose-breasted grosbeak—eastern
Black-headed grosbeak—western
Evening grosbeak—northernmost states and mountains in west
Blue grosbeak—southernmost states

BUNTINGS

Three species, difficult to attract to feeders: millet, mixed birdseed, thistle, bread crumbs

Indigo bunting—eastern
Lazuli bunting—western
Painted bunting—extreme southeast and southwest

FINCHES, PINE GROSBEAK, AND ROSY FINCH

Five species, first three easy to attract and common at bird feeders: sunflower, thistle seed, millet

Purple finch—widespread, chiefly northern states
Cassin's finch—western
House finch—widespread, western and introduced in east
Pine grosbeak—widespread, northern and mountains in west
Rosy finch—mountains in west (three races)

PINE SISKIN AND GOLDFINCHES

Three species, easy to attract: sunflower, thistle, millet

Pine siskin—northern and far west
American goldfinch—widespread
Lesser goldfinch—southwest

TOWHEES

Three species, vary from easy to attract to being too shy to come: sunflower, mixed birdseed, suet

Green-tailed towhee—far western
Rufous-sided towhee—widespread
Brown towhee—far western

JUNCOS

One species, readily attracted to feeders: sunflower, millet, bakery products

Dark-eyed junco—northern and far western (four races)

TRUE SPARROWS

Five species, vary from indifferent to easily attracted: sunflower, thistle, millet

Chipping sparrow—widespread
Field sparrow—eastern
White-crowned sparrow—far western
Fox sparrow—far western
Song sparrow—widespread

HOW TO PREVENT BIRD SEED FROM SPOILING IN SUMMER

Many people are unaware of the fact that bird seeds spoil or deteriorate much faster in the warm weather of summer than they do in winter. To have a successful summer feeding program, we need to take this fact into account and take proper precautions.

A. Primary causes of spoilage
  (1) Oil in seeds having a high oil content has a tendency to become rancid in hot weather. Therefore special precautions should be taken with high oil seeds such as sunflower, safflower, thistle (niger) and peanuts. Sunflower and safflower, because of the insulating effect of their hulls, withstand warm temperatures better than the others.
  (2) Bird seeds are susceptible to molds and mildew in warm, humid weather. This is particularly true of cracked corn. Whole corn is better able to withstand summer weather conditions.
  (3) Insect larvae, present in all oil-bearing seeds, may develop from worm to adult state if the seeds are stored for too long a time (a month or longer) in containers or bags. The most serious pest is the grain moth (*Sitotroga cerealella*). As the larvae of this moth develops inside the seed, the kernel (the part birds eat) is destroyed.

B. Hazards of spoiled seeds
  Seeds that are rancid, moldy or worm-infested are poorer in vitamins, proteins and other nutrients than fresh seeds. If rancid or moldy, the seeds could represent a health hazard to birds.
  Fortunately, birds can nearly always be depended upon not to eat spoiled seeds. This is the main reason why birds sometimes desert feeders in summer. There is nothing wrong with their appetites; the seeds are at fault.

C. Precautions
  (1) Allow birds to eat up your winter supply of bird seeds before warm weather comes. Then order fresh supplies.

(2) Avoid buying large quantities of seeds at one time and purchase seeds from a reliable dealer. In the case of thistle and sunflower meats, buy no more than a 2 to 3 weeks' supply at a time. For other seeds, buy no more than a month's supply at a time.

(3) Store seeds in as cool and dry a place as possible.

(4) As a rule, buy only 10 or 20 lb. bags and, if space is available, store in the refrigerator or freezer.

(5) If you keep seed in metal garbage can type containers outside or in the garage, hang a Shell No-Pest strip in container to avoid problems from insect larvae.

(6) If the container is kept outside, secure the top so that squirrels, raccoons, and others cannot gain access.

(7) So that seeds do not spoil in feeders, put out smaller quantities in summer and refill more often.

Remember that fresh, high-quality seeds are best for birds and will keep them coming back to your feeders. If in doubt about the freshness or quality of the seeds, it is best to dispose of them and obtain a new supply.

SOME MAJOR REHABILITATION CENTERS

Alaska Raptor Rehab Center
P.O. Box 2151
Sitka, AK 99835
Phone: (907) 747-8662

Alabama Wildlife Rescue Service
2107 Marlboro Avenue
Birmingham, AL 35226
Phone: (205) 320-6189

Alexander Lindsay Junior Museum
1901 First Avenue
Walnut Creek, CA 94596
Phone: (415) 935-1978

California Marine Mammal Center
Marin Headlands
Golden Gate National Rec. Area
Fort Cronkite, CA 94965
Phone: (415) 331-7325

International Bird Rescue
Aquatic Park
Berkley, CA 94710
Phone: (415) 841-9086

Marin Wildlife Center
76 Albert Park Lane
San Rafael, CA 94915
Phone: (415) 454-6961

Monterey County SPCA
P.O. Box 3058
Monterey, CA 93942
Phone: (408) 373-2631

Peninsula Humane Society
12 Airport Boulevard
San Mateo. CA 94401
Phone: (415) 573-3720

Project Wildlife
764 S. Glen Oaks Drive
Alpine, CA 92001
Phone: (916) 225-9453

Wildlife Rehabilitation Service
524 Delaware Street
Fairfield, CA 94533
Phone: (707) 429-4295

Birds of Prey Rehab Foundation
P.O. Box 261145
Lakewood, CO 80226
Phone: (303) 232-0140

The Mews Raptor
Rehabilitation Center
Cox Road
Portland, CT 06480
Phone: (203) 342-2672

Tri-State Bird Rescue & Research
2920 Duncan Road
Wilmington, DE 19808
Phone: (302)994-7578

Care & Rehabilitation of Wildlife
Sanibel Captiva Road
Captiva Island, FL 33924
Phone: (813) 472-3644

Suncoast Seabird Sanctuary
18328 Gulf Shores Boulevard
Indian Shores, FL 33535
Phone: (813) 391-6211

Treehouse WIldlife
Rt 1 Box 125E
Brighton, IL 62012
Phone: (618) 372-8092

Willowbrook Wildlife Haven
525 S. Park Boulevard
Glen Ellyn, IL 60137
Phone: (708) 790-4900

Chesapeake Wildlife Sanctuary
17308 Queen Anne Bridge Road
Bowie, MD 20716
Phone: (301) 390-7010

New England Wildlife Center
146A Justice Cushing Highway
Hingham, MA 02043
Phone: (617) 749-1248

Raptor Research & Rehab Program
295 Animal Science
Veterinary Medicine Building
1988 Fitch Avenue
St. Paul, MN 55108
Phone: (612) 624-4969

**Raptor Rehab and
Propagation Project**
Tyson Research Center
P.O. Box 193
Eureka, MO 63025
Phone: (314) 938-6193

Wildlife Rehab League
2450 Battleground Avenue
Greensboro, NC 27408
Phone: (919) 299-2827

The Raptor Trust
1390 White Bridge Road
Millington, NJ 07946
Phone: (201) 647-2353

Lifeline For Wildlife
Stoney Point, NY 10980
Phone: (914) 429-0180

Volunteers For Wildlife
P.O. Box 427
Cold Spring Harbor, NY 11724
Phone: (516) 367-4468

Brukner Nature Center
5995 Horseshoe Bend Road
Troy, OH 45373
Phone: (513) 698-6493

Wildlife Rescue, Inc.
c/o Natural Science Center
401 Deep Eddy Avenue
Austin, TX 78703
Phone: (512) 472-9453

The Wildlife Center of Virginia
P.O. Box 98
Weyers Cave, VA 24486
Phone: (703) 234-9453

Vermont Raptor Center
Vermont Institute of
Natural Science
Woodstock, VT 05091
Phone: (802) 457-2779

Progressive Animal Welfare
Wildlife Rehabilitation Center
P.O. Box 5574
Lynnwood, WA 98046
Phone: (206) 325-7242

Northwoods Wildlife Center
Highway 70 West
Minocqua, WI 54548
Phone: (715) 356-7400

**Wildlife Animal Rehabilitation
Co-op**
41541 N. Humboldt Avenue
Milwaukee, WI 53212
Phone (414) 961-0310

Owl Rehabilitation
Research Foundation
Rt 1 Vineland Station
Ontario, Canada LOR 2EO
Phone: (416) 562-5986

BIRD FEEDING GUIDES

Dennis, John V. *A Complete Guide To Bird Feeding.* New York: Alfred A. Knopf, 1975.

Dennis, John V. *Beyond The Bird Feeder.* New York: Alfred A. Knopf, 1981.

Dennis, John V. *The Wildlife Gardener.* New York: Alfred A. Knopf, 1985.

Harrison, George H. *The Backyard Birdwatcher.* New York: Simon and Schuster, 1979.

Pistorius, Alan *The Country Journal Book Of Birding And Bird Attraction.* New York: W. W. Norton & Company, 1981.

Stokes, Donald W. & Lillian Q. *The Bird Feeder Book.* Boston, Toronto: Little, Brown & Company, 1987.

Stokes, Donald W. & Lillian Q. *A Guide To Bird Behavior: Vols. I & II.* Boston, Toronto: Little, Brown & Company, 1983.

FIELD GUIDES

Farrand, John Jr. *The Audubon Handbooks.* New York: McGraw-Hill Book Company, 1988.

Field Guide To The Birds Of North America. National Geographic Society, 1983.

Peterson, Roger Tory. *A Field Guide To The Birds.* Boston: Houghton Mifflin, 1961.

Peterson, Roger Tory. *A Field Guide To Western Birds.* Boston: Houghton Mifflin, 1961.

Robbins, Chandler S., Bertel Bruun, & Herbert S. Zim. *A Guide To Field Identification: Birds Of North America.* New York: Golden Press, 1966.

VIDEO CASSETTES

Attracting Birds To Your Backyard. With Roger Tory Peterson, 60 minutes. Full color. Produced & Directed by Michael Godfrey of Nature Science Network, 1986. (VHS or Beta).

Audubon Society Video Guides to Birds of North America.
5 Cassetts Volumes. Full Color. Produced & Directed by Michael Godfrey. Mastervision. New York. 1988. (VHS or Beta)

Bluebird Trails: How to Start & Maintain a Bluebird Nest Trail.
Full Color. Approximately 25 minutes. Produced & Directed by Boz Metzdorf of Birds' Eye View Productions. Afton, Minnesota. 1989. (VHS)

Hummingbirds Up Close. 58 minutes. Full Color. Produced & Directed by Michael Godfrey of Nature Science Network, 1986. (VHS or Beta).

Jewels of Blue: The Story of the Eastern Bluebird. Full Color 30 minutes. Produced & Directed by Boz Metzdorf of Birds' Eye View Productions. Afton, Minnesota. 1988. (VHS).

BIRD FEEDING SUPPLIES

Audubon Workshop, Inc.
1501 Paddock Dr., Northbrook, IL 60062, (708) 729-6660
Complete catalog of Summer and All-Year-Round bird feeding products and services. Free catalog to readers of this book.

INDEX